# DEVELOPING CHARACTER
*And*
# CREATING CHARACTERS

*Loraine Dennis Trollope*

Order this book online at www.trafford.com
or email orders@trafford.com

Most Trafford titles are also available at major online book retailers.

Printed in the United States of America.

ISBN: 978-1-4269-9492-0 (sc)
ISBN: 978-1-4269-9493-7 (e)

Trafford rev. 10/12/2011

 www.trafford.com

North America & International
toll-free: 1 888 232 4444 (USA & Canada)
phone: 250 383 6864 ♦ fax: 812 355 4082

# CONTENTS

# PROLOGUE

Where do we go from here is the question that everyone has to face multiple times in his lifetime? The answer might be hidden in the past. To know where we are headed could be couched in incidents that took place in the early years. Looking back on the trail that has been traveled indicates what can be expected on the road ahead. Introspection is an important exercise in this or any other case. It allows us to document some of the guiding factors in our lives. Every life is important and every person has a story to tell. Unfortunately many people die leaving no story to outline the their life's defining moments. As time passes not only what they have done is gone but also gone is their memory. I have talked with many people relating anecdotes of incidents that have been my experience and stories related to me from relatives who lived them. Most who hear the stories say, "You should write a book." Well, here it is! This is the first attempt at that project. This is my story but, in a way, it is their story. The main scope of the book is to document growing up on a ranch/farm is Wibaux County during the 1940's-1950's and how those experiences developed character and created characters in the rugged peoples who lived, worked and died there.

Years ago my father realized the value of leaving a book. He spent several months in our old Montana ranch house writing a fictional account of what may, I believe, were some of his adventures as a cowboy, real or imagined. Somehow, the manuscript was lost until a few years later when it was found in its unfinished condition tucked away in an old magazine rack. It is interesting that the story was not finished. Why it was not finished is a question left for us to ponder. It just could be that even writing a fictional account of a person's life may be too painful a task for many people to fully carry out. At any rate, his story forms as an addendum to this book.

My great grandfather having fought in the Civil War as a teenager realized the need to record his story. His manuscript was written on tablets in his North Dakota farmhouse during the late 1920's. Following his death in 1935 it was his daughter who in 1957 gave the document to Byron Abernathy who edited and published great grandfather's writings. This book of his has since become an important historical document of the exploits of a young Civil War soldier, "Private Elisha Stockwell Sees The Civil War."

Histories of the Amunrud and Stockwell branches of the family tree have surfaced. Some of which are extremely well documented and printed in both hard cover and soft cover form. Other family members are in the process of gathering information concerning the Trollope families. These comprise family trees that outline early American adventures of those families. These writings are also filled with pathos, success and short-term failures, which were ultimately overcome.

All of these writings give insight into individual lives providing us with a window into the past. These views can be of value in learning what were the experiences of these hardy people. By reviewing the factors of failure and success that they encountered, we can learn valuable lessons from what they endured. Whether the lessons are relevant to the current time and situation is for the reader to decide. Whatever the case may be they provide a mirror that may reflect our own lives.

While these stories may be of value, a caution should be given to the reader. The incidents are written from memory and give only limited perspectives as to events that may have taken place. In many cases, there are certain to be mistakes, inaccurate perceptions and misconceptions throughout this book. There is always a temptation on the part of the writer to editorialize and expand tidbits for the purpose of adding color to make the read more interesting if not more entertaining. Hopefully, the enticement to go beyond the real story will be minimized. This approach should be acceptable to the reader because the intent of this writing is not to document history so much as it is to place the participants in history to define the elements that later were important in the development of their character. Sharing the joys and challenges of their lives is the purpose of taking both the writer's and reader's time.

In any Prologue, it is appropriate to thank all of those individuals whose help, witness, and guidance made the story possible. The typist, editor, publisher are all recognized in most Prologues. Many writers will dedicate the book to important persons involved in the story, its development and its production. To accomplish this task in this case would be very difficult because of the large number of people who are responsible for the content and scope of the book. To dedicate or thank all of those who were instrumental in its writing would take as many pages as the book itself. What has been written is a compilation of each person's contribution. It is for this reason as those contributors read the book they will find their own recognition and our appreciation in this cooperative endeavor. A big thanks goes out to everyone involved.

Special Note:
The cover of this book shows Grandfather Dan Stockwell on his tractor with his brother Len Stockwell on the plow as they broke sod in their farming operations. The picture is hazy, cloudy and nondescript, just as is history in many cases leaving much to the interpretation of the observer.

## EARLY YEARS:

The early years are probably the most difficult to relate due to the long period of time that has passed. It seems that over the years there have been a never-ending parade of characters that made their way across the prairies of Western North Dakota and Eastern Montana. Each one was seeking an opportunity to obtain his or her stake in the territory and was willing to work for a better life. They came in immigrant cars, wagons, and on horseback. Sadly, there are very few of these rugged pioneers left with us today. Their absence adds to the difficulty of providing a comprehensive picture of the life and times of that era which included the late 1800's and early 1900's. Our part of the story picks up during the late 1930's through the 1960's. It is during this time period that probably as much change came to this territory as had been experienced in the previous several hundred years.

# BLUE MOUNTAIN COTTONWOOD COMMUNITY:

Blue Mountain is a mountain located just north of Wibaux Montana and the Cottonwood Community. It is an outcropping of sandstone that can be seen for miles. The elevation of the Mountain is 2,881 ft. It "towers" above the surrounding terrain by only a few hundred feet. Yet many times during the day we would turn our eyes to the north and see its beautiful blue color. It served many purposes. One could readily determine their orientation as it was always to the north. Even today, some of us who are seeking their position think of north as Blue Mountain. Blue Mountain became our sense of identity. We were from Blue Mountain Country. It was a rallying point for the homesteaders in the area. It was a point of reference for all.

One other point of reference on the road north of Wibaux is a series of hills (mountains?) called Four Buttes. This outcropping has an elevation of 2,802 ft. Nearby is a ridge known as the Divide Road, which is approximately five miles, or so long dividing the country east to west. It appears that this divide separates drainage to Beaver Creek to the east and Cottonwood Creek to the west. Water from Beaver Creek drains to the Little Missouri River and Cottonwood Creek drains to the Yellowstone River.

Traveling east from Four Buttes on the Divide Road take the right of the Y road at that location and travel down to Beaver Creek and you will find the old W Bar ranch that Pierre Wibaux founded in the 1880's. The only building left standing is the old horse barn. It is of stone construction and housed the cowboy's horses. Not wanting to start a major fundraising task, but it would be very significant to the history of the County if the barn could be repaired and the ranch house rebuilt. It probably is as important to the settlement of North Dakota and Montana as the complex at Medora. History not preserved is history lost.

For those who are driving north of Wibaux along Hwy 261 two other important points of reference include Lone Tree and the "Y". Unfortunately, Lone Tree, an old cottonwood tree located just north of Four Buttes, died in the 1940's only to be washed away from site in the 1950's. It no longer exists. A similar story of the demise of the "Y" took place during the 1960's when the road was straightened out destroying the familiar "Y" in the road. Pay no attention to these details because area residents still know where they used to be and their locations are frequently referred to when giving directions. Oh, while we are at it, the old Been School is gone as is the Been Post Office. About the only early landmark that exists is the Been Cemetery. It is located just NE of the old John Trollope place. Oops, there is one landmark still visible and that is the old Cottonwood Hall, which is located along Cottonwood Creek and just north of the hill that previously was occupied by the Williams School. The school, of course, is gone but it still remains an important spot for gauging your location if you knew where it once stood. Across the fence from the Cottonwood hall are the remains of an old log cabin, which is probably known as the Williams Place. These points of reference mean little to those who have lost their way or who never traveled this way before. But they will live on forever in the hearts of those old timers whose very lives revolved around these landmarks.

The old Been Cemetery lies quietly atop a hill just northeast of John Trollope's ranch. I believe that the Trollope's donated this plot of land (115ft. X 140ft.) to the community to be used as a cemetery. SE 1/4 Sec. 22-17N-R59E. There are eleven graves included in the plot: "Jesse Appley, a hired man of Trollope, who drowned 16 July 1916; J.W. Wymore; Henrieta Wymore the last person buried in the cemetery; Sara L. Plavle 1873-1913; George Stedman 1921; Jesse Stedman 1922; John Clark Baby? Girl about 3-4 years old buried in a full size grave; John Been?; Trollope Baby; Lowell Johnston who was Ethel's husband; Winfield Jul 27 1914-Oct 3, 1919."

# SPECIAL NOTES THAT TELL IT ALL;

Growing up in Montana was a great experience. I will never forget summer rains that settled dust, rainbows, springtime flowers, crocus, gumbo lilies and wild roses. New born calves, newly sheared sheep, horses, foals, new lambs, baby chicks, green grass, choke cherries, wild plums, gooseberries, meadow larks, magpies, sparrows, crows, owls, hawks, porcupines, deer, antelope, snakes, raccoons, bobcats, rabbits, skunks, fox, blue skies, cumulus clouds, thunderhead clouds, fresh air smells, branding fires, quiet times, rising creeks, washed out fence lines, melting snow, new ice on the creek, sounds in the night, crickets, stars, moon, blackness, welcome sunlight, rhubarb, growing grain, pig weeds, Indian tobacco, visiting salesmen, preacher's rounds, relatives visiting. 4-H meetings, red grass, buffalo grass, creeping jenny, thistles, horse radish, sunflowers, elm trees, Russian olive groves, threshing machines, horse drawn hayracks, water buckets with dippers, wash bowls, Ivory soap, Lava pumice soap, gasoline smells, the bawl of a distant calf or cow, the clump-clump of horse's hooves, ammonia smell in the hen house, flies in the barn, chicken mites, baler twine, the smell of dinner cooking on the stove, newly waxed linoleum floors, warmth from a wood burning kitchen stove, smell of tilled soil, worms, bones, dried cow hides, moss and algae growing on the water tank, hunting, target shooting, bedtime and cold sheets, soft summer breezes, Blue Mountain, creeks, coulees, bunk houses, haystacks, sagging barb wire fences, grain bins, shops, swimming holes, old wells, hope for tomorrow, empty spaces at the dinner table, big family holiday meals, Paris Green, potato bugs, sheep dip, 2-4D pesticide, linen water bags, rusty nails, broken glass, sunflowers, wild onions, bullheads & carp, sick people, happy people, old people, new babies, noisy kids, dust, barbed-chicken-sheep-telephone and baling wire. Nobby tires, inner tube patching, tire chains, missing fenders, blue smoke, noisy mufflers, bare seat springs, steaming radiators, broken speedometers, bent license plates, and cracked windshields.

# HOMELIFE:

Being a homesteader and the generation that followed was a most exciting if not a totally comfortable existence by today's standards. Our farms and ranches had no electricity. Kerosene lamps and Coleman high-octane "white" gasoline lanterns provided light for homes and outbuildings. The homes were quite dark and many of the rooms did not even have any illumination due to the cost of fuel, lanterns and the safety hazards that open flames presented to young children. It was very dark during the nights and one did not venture far outside as a result. When you did have to make emergency trips to the outhouse, you stepped high and did not spend too much time out there. Are you scared of the dark? Yes. I still am to a certain extent even today. If it wasn't ghosts and goblins it was rattlesnakes and potential wild animals that concerned youngsters and oldsters as well.

In our case, water for drinking, bathing, and laundry purposes had to be hauled home in galvanized cream cans loaded in the back of a pick up truck. These were filled at Grandma Stockwell's water well or at the City Service Garage garden hose in downtown Wibaux. Cans had to be unloaded manually from the pickup truck. This proved to be a real chore. At about 8.35 pounds per gallon, a 10-gallon water can might weigh up to about 84 pounds. The eight-gallon cans weighed about 67 pounds and those pesky five-gallon cream cans filled with this precious liquid totaled about 42 pounds not including the weight of the container. Water would freeze if left outside during subzero temperatures so cans were kept in the warm kitchen at those times. In the summer the water cans were stored in the lean-to shed on the north side of the house where it was cooler and out of the sun. Another source of water was the rain barrel, which was located under the eaves on the low-sloped roof of the farmhouse. Of course, we had water well for livestock but the water was so laced with iron and other minerals, that it was not potable for household use. Left for any period of time the water turned a bright orange color due to the formation of iron oxide. The washstand containing a basin and water pail was located in the corner of the kitchen. An enamelware dipper was used to dip water into the washbasin for shaving and washing up before meals. When thirsty, everyone drank from the same dipper, which was retuned back into the pail after each use. The washstand drain had a five-gallon bucket for collecting the wash water, which was subsequently tossed out into the yard providing a beneficial effect of settling the dust and scattering the chickens. Hand soap was usually Lava pumice stone type because it efficiently removed accumulated grease, fuel and paint from hands and even sometimes from faces. Ivory bar soap was a constant companion in cleaning up for supper. The slogan "99 44/100's Pure" sold most everybody in the county on its effectiveness besides it floated. If hot water was needed, a lime-encrusted teakettle was always on the cook stove and could be counted on to serve up its steaming liquid. The drying hand towel hung on a rack nearby. This towel was usually made from a corn or flour sack and was of a coarse texture. Unfortunately it was usually wet, wreaking of gasoline and stained with axle grease. Overhead was the medicine cabinet which housed old Gillette brass double edged shaving razors, shaving mug, tooth brushes, mentholatum, iodine, aspirin, band-Aids, and maybe some bolts and small screws the origins of which could not be determined or were long forgotten but which must have been important at some time.

Saturday night brought the weekly bath for everyone in the house. The galvanized bathtub hung on the north wall of the house ready to be carted in and placed near the oil stove. It was filled with hot water from a five gallon cream can, which had been placed on the oil stove to thaw and provide bath water. Now, that water was very hot to begin with. It did cool as successive individuals climbed into the tub to be scoured down. More hot water was added as needed. Soap in eyes caused a burning sensation until cleared away with clean water or from tears. Dreading the climb out of the warm water into the cool house brought many a chill and considerable shivering along with chattering teeth. Floors in the home were always cold and there were times when icy drafts of air entered the home through loose fitting doors and windows. Homes lacked good insulation. Snow was banked up against the house to a height of about four feet in order to ward off the northwestern cold blasts of Canadian air. The wind would howl as the drifting snow piled up around the buildings.

When nature called for a trip to the outhouse during the winter season, it was answered by a mad dash outside and the visit was a very brief period of time. During the winter the temperatures sometimes were five to twenty five below zero. Winds of thirty miles per hour were not uncommon. These privies or "backhouses" have been the brunt of many a poem, story, and anecdote but in whatever descriptive form they took, the chill involved with their use would not be soon forgotten. Summertime trips to these sanitary facilities were not a problem unless it was at night with no light to guide the way. The rutted trail was fraught with tripping hazards and don't forget, "watch out for rattlesnakes!"

Growing up on the farm brought excitement and danger. One night our hired man, Frankie Johnston was babysitting us three boys aged about 3-4-5 years of age. He was serving dinner as one of us boys pulled the window curtain over into the gasoline lantern that was sitting on the kitchen table. The curtain was ignited, flames raced up the wall, until Frankie quickly pulled it down. He burned his hands but in so doing saved the day.

Some years later kerosene lanterns were knocked over igniting straw in two of our barns. These little blazes were put out quickly.

Iceboxes were found in almost every homestead kitchen. It was a common wooden cabinet lined with metal. Blocks of ice were placed in the upper portion of the unit, which cooled the air keeping the contents of the interior relatively cool. Ice was obtained during the winter season from frozen ponds or dams and was stored in a root cellar located in the front yard of the house. The blocks of ice were packed tightly in straw and sawdust for insulation from the hot summer heat. This kept the ice in good condition for several months.

Ice was used to make ice cream, float watermelons, and to cool food in the icebox. As the ice melted, water accumulated in the pan below on the bottom shelf. The cooling cabinet had a flat pan that was used to store cream. One day we kids got into the bottom cabinet and spilled all of the cream. I am not certain if we cried over spilled cream but in later years we were taught not to cry over spilled milk.

The oil burner stoves used for heating the farmhouse posed fire hazards. Sometimes heat exchangers would be red hot in the attempt to address the subzero temperatures that Montana winters brought. What prevented this overheated condition from causing a fuel oil explosion is nothing short of a miracle. During heavy usage, the stove would "boom" and make menacing sounds. One time, we had a fire caused by one of these stoves out on the ranch, however. It was a chimney fire, as I recall. We lost a lot of our books, memorabilia, and toys as result fire and water damage. Another time we had a back draft in the stove causing the stovepipe to separate and the whole house was filled with oily, black soot balls. We had to remove furniture from the house and chase this soot with a broom in an attempt to clean up the mess. No vacuum cleaners in those days.

Washday was not one of my favorite days. Mom would pull out the old gasoline engine powered Maytag washing machine, fill it with water, and start the engine that powered the appliance. She would add naphtha and hard soap to the water and dump in the clothes. When fully washed, the clothes would be run through the wringer to remove excess water. The wringer was constructed of two rubber rollers having heavy tension springs. This process readied the clothes for posting on the clothesline for drying in the sunshine. Two problems with this operation. The house was filled with gasoline fumes and on at least one occasion, I caught my arm in the wringer. As luck would have it, there was a release that popped the rollers apart after some spinning operations on the arm. Painful. Now I know what it means when someone who is tired saying that they feel like they have been run through a wringer.

The old wood-burning cook stove was a godsend. It would heat the kitchen and some other parts of the house. We would stoke it up with scrap wood obtained from our woodpile, which was located just north of the house. Sometimes locally obtained lignite coal was used in this stove. When the ashes left from this soft coal were hauled out, we found "clinkers" of glass, bolts and nails from the coal and wood. Today the woodpile is gone but the nearby ash dump probably is still there. Friction taped axes used in chopping wood were common tools found around the farmhouse kitchen, as were coal buckets and ash shovels. There is nothing like the warmth of an old kitchen stove in the winter. On one side of the stove was a reservoir for heating water. An old lime encrusted teakettle was also always on the stove. Overhead above the burners/griddle were located the ovens in which fresh baked goods were kept warm. The large cooking oven located near the floor was where the real cooking was done. Baked breads, roasted meats, and stews came from this heated box.

Coal could be obtained from creek beds where lignite soft coal could be found. This coal was wet and required drying before it could be burned. It was quite sulfurous and was not of the high quality hard coal briquettes that could be purchased in town. Digging coal from the creek banks was a task. Usually a team of horses and a wagon was brought to the site to haul the coal home. It seems that each farm had a small supply of dynamite, caps and fuse stored for use in blasting out coal from dirt banks along the coulees and streams.

Cold weather brought its own changes. The REA (Rural Electrification Administration) power lines and telephone lines would "sing" as the wires would tighten up in the chill. In the depth of winter the howling of the wind can be remembered and the sounds of the wires recalled almost nightly as we hunkered down in our snug beds. Frost on the windows and wind blown snow around loose fitting windows had to be contended with. Harold Warp Flex-O-Glass cellophane clear material was nailed over the windows in the chicken house and the farmhouse. This material proved to be quite effective in winterizing the buildings but drafts were common. The installation of genuine storm windows was still off in the future for many Montana ranch houses. The walls were not well insulated and rooms located far from the kitchen stove or the oil stove in the living room tended to be chilly. Heavy blue paper was used to cover the board walls between the bare studded walls in the house. Sometimes ordinary newspapers were used in the place of the blue paper to insulate the interior walls where there was no interior sheathing provided. At other times lath and plaster was placed over the studded walls on the interior of the more up to date farmhouses. Most times Celotex fiberboard was nailed over the studs and painted. Exterior walls had common wooden ship lap covering. Some mornings the house would be so cold that there would be ice in the water bucket in the kitchen especially if the fire in the stove went out. When called for breakfast in the early morning hours, we would show up in our stocking feet, which were promptly placed on the wooden members of the old oak pedestal table to escape the cold floor. Buyers of old antique kitchen tables today take note that the legs of these tables are many times scuffed and worn from this activity. The practice resting feet on the table legs continues today even though our modern kitchens have floors that are toasty warm. Old habits are hard to break.

Floors in these old ranch-farm houses were composed of simple wooden boards covered with rolled linoleum covering. There are few surfaces that are colder than linoleum in the winter. Gold Seal and Johnson & Johnson floor wax came on the market proving to be a boon to housekeeping in the ranch house. These waxes when applied to linoleum brought a sheen that even today is difficult to duplicate in the finest office buildings. In unheated rooms, linoleum floor covering edges would curl up. Installation of metal strips nailed down in the doorways and elsewhere was necessary to limit tripping hazards and damage to the floor covering. To have wool carpeting was an unheard of luxury in ranch homes and elsewhere with the exception of a very few homes occupied by wealthier people. The only carpeted floors that I can remember seeing during those times were in the Rose Movie Theater in Glendive. Oh my, how plush those thick red carpets were.

To receive RFD (Rural Free Delivery) USPO mail was a great treat. I remember everyone watching for the mailman to come. One time Dad ordered out a tap and die tool set for the shop. It was delivered by mail and I carried it from the mailbox to the house. It was very heavy and it was difficult to transport. It is kind of amazing that as a kid of four or five, I was allowed to walk over to the main road, cross the road, open the mailbox and walk back the distance, which would have been about two city blocks. Must have been a surprise to Mom. Not much mail was received during those years. This was in the era prior to junk mail. We subscribed to few magazines. There was the weekly Wibaux Pioneer Gazette, however. Occasional letters were received. Letter postage was three cents and post card postage was one cent. Mail usually was placed in a cotton sack that was fashioned from used flour sacks, placed in the metal mailbox along the county gravel road to await either the addressee or for the mailman who drove by on his rounds. The sack kept letters from blowing around. Have you heard the term "mail bag?" This was what we called these bags. Sure enough we can almost see the postman riding along on his open air Jeep making stops at each mailbox.

Cotton flour and chicken feed sacks also provided needed fabric for the housewife's dress, aprons and tea towels used for drying dishes. We kids on these fabrics did some embroidery work on during the wintertime.

Late at night in the old farmhouse, mice could be heard running in the ceiling space above. Mousetraps were somewhat effective in their control but it wasn't until a new rat and mouse poison made its entry into the drug and hardware stores that the problem rodents were controlled. We would take the poison, add oats, and place in toilet paper packets. These packets were then either placed or thrown into attic spaces for consumption by those bothersome critters with great effectiveness. This rat poison was very powerful in eliminating the noisy rodents overhead while one was trying to sleep. In later years a similar poison was prescribed by doctors as a blood thinner to prevent blood clots in human circulatory systems.

Beneath our ranch house was a dugout cellar, which contained fruit jars, cardboard boxes and other knickknacks having little value. The sides of the cellar had caved in and in some places were held in place by sticks cut from tree branches from the nearby coulees. These were woven into an earthen bunker in an attempt to stabilize crumbling dirt walls.

## UNFORGETTABLE CHARACTERS:

Our town had interesting characters. One of whom comes to mind was Sam. He used to walk around town with a parrot on his shoulder and many times he could be found frequenting the barbershop. Another fellow was Hjalmer, a sheepherder who moved to town and occupied the main street barbershop building in later years. He collected agates and all manner of rocks from his sheep ranch south of town. He polished these stones in a rotating tub using a polishing compound. The rocks came out in beautiful gemstone like condition. He was quite a geologist and had studied rocks for years. Hjalmer lived in the back of the store. A third fellow that I remember was "Happy." He came from a historic family who once worked for Pierre Wibaux. He would trudge around town very slowly pulling a small wagon filled with stuff. His family lived on a ranch north of town before moving to Wibaux. Happy, while walking out in the prairie one very hot day was encountered by Dad inquiring where he was headed with his fishing pole and can of worms. He said that he was going fishing on the Yellowstone River. The River was probably 20 miles distant. Imagine trudging all of those miles to fish in the Yellowstone. I never quite forgot this fellow as well as the others in the community. They were determined and had definite goals which they were going to attain. Another unforgettable fellow was a farmer who was building a sailboat in his barnyard. I stopped to see him one day and his wife pointed out that he was behind the barn. When I rounded the barn I saw a large wooden boat in about a 75% completed condition. The country had not seen rain in months and farmland was parched. When asked what he was doing, he stated that he was building a boat to sail down the Mississippi River. The

River was located some hundreds of miles distant. Unbelievable or irrational as this seemed, it was his goal. I could only equate this situation to Noah building his Ark. Stories about the characters who lived in our town and countryside are numerous. Hank with his team of horses and wagon would make deliveries of freight around town. Kids would hitch rides on his wagon and were treated to a tour of the town. Other times Hank would be grading gravel streets in town using an old horse drawn grader. This ride for the kids was slower but did provide other thrills, especially when a slip and fall onto the iron framework occurred. This provided a painful experience on at least one outing. It is unfortunate that more space cannot be devoted to more of the "goings on" with these hardworking people. Maybe somebody else will expand these snippets in another book. I mention them here to show the witness that these people gave us all in showing their determination, commitment in working toward their goals and the effect they had on all of us.

## SNAKES:

Granddad Trollope mentioned one time that they had gone out to dynamite a rattlesnake den, which was located in the pasture. Snakes congregate together in the fall of the year forming large balls of snakes in lairs beneath the Montana sod. These reptiles are intertwined and are dormant during the cold winter months only to emerge when the weather turns warmer. Granddad and some of the boys went out on one occasion bringing along blasting material for the purpose of dynamiting one of the dens. The blasting material was set in a hole, the fuse lit and the sod soon erupted in a volcanic-type display. After the noise had subsided, they looked up into the sky to find snakes flying through the air like ropes. All was fine until they started falling on the ground all around. Somehow the story ended there. We can only surmise as to the outcome. Needless to say, this stunt was not repeated in successive years. End of story.

Another story about rattlesnake harvesting or eradication has just surfaced. It involved the placement of pipes lying vertically on rocky hillsides near snake dens. These wily critters would emerge from the den, enter the pipe and slide down the slippery interior of the tubes depositing themselves below into a 55-gallon barrel. These snakes were then, evidently, sold to an area processor who used them to provide deer hunter scent masking liquids for deer hunters.

Mom looked into a window on one of our empty granaries on the Quinlog place and spied a rattlesnake on the dirt floor. She crawled through into the bin to kill it with an ax. When she hit the ground she feared that there could be two or three other snakes in this enclosed space. Now began the battle royale. Mom came through unscathed and there ended up being only the single reptile occupying the space with her. Chalk up one less critter with rattles and one grateful lady that his whole gang was not there in the bin.

One time we were pitching bundles of wheat straw into a hayrack at harvest time. Beneath one of the shocks was a large rattlesnake. He did not present overly aggressive tendencies but we took care to limit possible injury from this reptile. One of us asked our hired hand, Thomse, who chewed snus if it was true that if tobacco juice was placed in a snake's mouth that they would bite themselves and die like we had seen in the movies. The response was that an experiment was in order. While forking the snake down, its mouth opened wide revealing fangs and a pure white interior. Tobacco was introduced into this gaping mouth using a straw. When turned loose, that critter reacted with a vengeance by striking out eventually biting himself. It is believed that the old wife's tale was correct because the he soon perished. An Internet search reveals that they are immune from their own venom. He must have expired from other trauma!

One time while walking along the gravel road we happened upon several baby rattle snakes. They were about the size of a pencil. We watched as they slithered along the hot, red scoria surfaced road. It was not until later that we found out that even these small snakes could evidently produce a serious bite. Luckily this time our curiosity was overcome by our healthy respect of all snakes big and small.

Many times rattlers were found in the roadway only to be run over by vehicles. This did not guarantee their demise even though they survived multiple attempts by the driver to repeat the roadway attack. It was discovered that if the vehicle's brakes were set in this endeavor that the snake would be killed sometimes emitting a noise resembling a sound similar to that of a breaking balloon. Safety personnel do not readily accept this practice, however.

There are stories concerning frozen snakes found in haystacks during the wintertime. Specific verification of these types of events was not to be found by this writer.

Sometimes rattlers would bite horses, dogs, or cattle causing painful results. We had one young neighbor who was bitten and suffered a tremendous swelling to her leg. I do not believe that she died of that attack.

Some farmsteads kept hogs because they were supposed to eat snakes. Never could verify this perception. As a preventative measure, Dad would advertise in the newspaper requesting free cats, which were put out in and around the farm buildings. Dad was the brunt of a lot of jokes concerning this practice until he made it known that cats ate mice which were one of the main food suppliers to rattle snakes. Cats meant no mice and no mice meant no snakes.

As kids we were always hammering on something. One time we killed a rattlesnake, cut it into pieces and nailed them to the shop floor. The nails are still there to be seen.

While we were always concerned over rattlesnake bites, I can report that in the twenty years spent in the Blue Mountain Country that no extremely dangerous encounters were noted but that probably is not the experience of everyone in the community. The snakes seen most times were lazily lying in the sun, crossing a road, caught in a ditch, or found docile in a vacant barn. These were not aggressive. I shudder to think that there were countless times we crawled under buildings or dived into caves that we built all the while being unconcerned over the possibility of other occupants. There are "dog days" in August in which a snake's skin is said to shed and in so doing, obscures his vision. It is at this time, they are said to strike out at anything that moves. Although this vignette is decried by the Internet and may not be true, August was a time when we paid special attention to our surroundings geared up for possible confrontations. At any rate we are very grateful that in the snake's evolution rattles were added to warn both humans and animals of their proximity.

## DYNAMITE:

Dynamite was always to be found around the ranch. It was used mainly to open clogged water springs on the prairie pastures. Being inquisitive kids we would go into Granddad's shop to see the mysterious contents therein. A coil of dynamite fuse was always available for our inspection. A short piece could easily be clipped off and set afire. Interesting how it would sputter and fume. We kids enjoyed perusing the old tools, feed sacks, mice, burlap bags, tarps, shotgun shells, paint, brushes, saddles, bridles, horse shoes, rope, old rifles, hay forks, shovels, and the list goes on. It was a great place to explore. No question about it that this building was a phantasmagoria of the exotic right there in Blue Mountain Country.

## HUNTING:

Granddad and his hired man were always out hunting bobcats, raccoons, skunks, and rabbits in the fall and winter seasons. They had a couple of well trained black and tan hunting hounds usually found curled up sunning themselves on some saddle blanket bed next to the bunkhouse. They would be set loose followed by John and Thomse bouncing along in the old green International pick up truck or trudging along on foot. By the barking of the dogs the hunters could tell what type of animal they were tracking. Happy yips meant rabbits. Whines meant porcupines or skunks. Raccoons and bobcats brought out entirely different yelps. The hunt usually ended up with a treed animal, dogs tearing into an animal or lost dogs as they trailed out of sight. It was always a sad day around the ranch whenever they ran off. In a couple of days they would show up a little worse for wear much to the jubilation of Thomse and John.

Everybody seems to be interested in the adopted wild animals we had. We had owls, deer, antelope, rabbits, birds, and hawks. All were let free after not thriving well in captivity. It was learned that if there was a nest of undesirable birds or animals these were open game. Crows, magpies, skunks, badgers, porcupines, snakes of all varieties, weasels, etc. were on our hunting lists continually. Now, those of us who read this commentary today, simply shudder at our treatment of the environment. The only salvation was that we weren't very good hunters, our weapons were at best ineffective and our quarry was smarter than us.

We hunted rabbits at night during the winter months. Our cars had spotlights with which we blinded rabbits congregated around haystacks and in rabbit holes dug in snow banks. We shot them with our 22 caliber rifles. Frozen rabbit carcasses were sold to a junk dealer in Beach, North Dakota for 0.65-0.75-$1.00 per each. Rabbit fur was used back east to make felt for hats and gloves. The meat was used to feed mink on fur farms back east. The mink needed wild meat to fully develop we were told.

As a youngster, Dad was out hunting. He spotted an animal that disappeared down a hole. He decided to blast away at it by placing the shotgun barrel into the hole. The gun recoiled upon discharge nearly breaking his thumb. Another stunt that was not repeated. Seems as though, we most generally learned by accident. Dad always said that we were not to point a gun at anything that we didn't want to shoot. He gave us kids only one bullet when we went out hunting. Guns were tools not playthings.

One night, there was a noise in the hen house. Dad got up, got his double barrel 12-gauge shotgun and went to see what was causing the fuss. He loaded and readied the gun forgetting that it had a sensitive hair trigger. With both hammers engaged he took one step forward on the porch and the old gun discharged accidentally causing everyone in the house to awaken with a start. Judging himself lucky not to be hit by the blast or shot Dad returned to the house and did not venture forth again that night. Funny, I don't remember losing any chickens. Probably a fox, coyote, or skunk were the invaders. Luckily everybody including the wild animals decided to retire for the rest of the night and the adventure was not repeated by either the chicken thieves or their brave defender.

## JUSTICE OF THE PEACE:

Sitting here just thinking of the many incidents involving Dad reminds me of one of the last telephone conversations I had with my ailing father. On the phone he sounded depressed, as he had been requested as Justice of the Peace to go to a local saloon to marry a Montana couple. I asked why he was reluctant to complete this task. He did not feel that tavern was a fitting place for a marriage to take place. I told him, "Think of it this way. It is about as close to church as a lot of them will ever come. It is up to you to be God's witness. Do your best." He said that he never thought of it that way and consequently felt better about it. The wedding went on as scheduled.

As a Justice of the Peace, Dad, was asked to marry a couple on horseback. He did draw the line on this plan and he did not perform the ceremony.

One courtroom story involved a biker who had been picked up on the highway by a Montana Highway Patrolman. He had been riding a fancy bike and he was all decked out in biker gear. On his hip was a .45 caliber pistol and there was a .30-.30 rifle in a scabbard near his saddlebags. A large bladed knife was slung at his hip. This hairy-faced offender swaggered into Dad's court with a sneer on his face and a vindictive, disrespectful attitude concerning the proceedings that were about to take place in the courtroom. Dad took control, advised that he was in charge and that if the defendant didn't straighten up his beard would be long and gray before he would ever emerge from the county jail. This caveat seemed to calm the miscreant. The case was heard, a fine was levied, and the offender left never to return. He took with him a small slice of Montana justice having left a sample of his largesse.

# HORSES:

Granddad Trollope's horses were put to work hauling hay and for other jobs around the farm. Gee-Haw was heard as the driver holding the reins would attempt to back the animals to align the wagon alongside of the granary. Driving those horses took real skill and patience, both of which Granddad and the horses possessed.

There is no experience like riding in an old hayrack being drawn by our favorite team. They almost became a part of the farmer's family. The hayrack with its steel wheels bouncing along the rutted prairie and bumpy rock road was spine jarring. Admonished to hold on, we kids would be tossed about with each turn and jerky motion. The sound of the coming entourage could be heard all the way to the house.

At an early age we kids acquired a Shetland pony. "Honey" was her name. This horse was quite unusual having been foundered by eating too much grain in her younger years. Her back legs were all crooked and deformed giving her a gait that could be best described as a waddle. This animal was about the most cantankerous critter I ever saw. She would run fast and then scrape along the house trying to "rub off" riders. A sweet work of art she was. I remember one ride, as I was holding on tight to her mane, she ran under the clothesline catching me under the chin and leaving me hanging there. I am not certain how I was rescued. It did make my throat sore. Little dogs and little horses have something in common, meanness. There were other times in which she would try to bite us. If there is a horse heaven she probably is not there.

Clell and John Trollope kidded around, as boys are wont to do. John roped a horse near a buffalo wallow and the captured steed began running. In the melee the saddle came off his horse. The roped bronco ran off pulling the still seated Granddad John through the wallow leaving his own horse behind. This proved to be a rough ride, no doubt! This probably proved to be damaging to the saddle also.

A hired man who was too lazy to take the 4-horse team to a gate in the fence decided to take a shortcut by cutting the top fence wire while holding down the other barbed wires intact. When two horses stepped over the fence, the wires snapped up. This spooked the remaining two horses and they began running along the fence, tearing the flesh from the horses closest to the fence. Two animals died in this tragic incident. I can just imagine the loud words that were spoken when the hired man returned to the house with only two of the four horses he started out with.

When Stanley was growing up, the roof on the homestead shack had holes in it. He would tell of lying in bed up seeing stars through it. Wooden shingles would be blown off during storms leaving bare parts of the roof. The ranch house was so cold that Stanley's ear froze one night. It probably would have been warmer in the horse barn.

## AXIOMS LEARNED:

Dad once gave this financial advice to us: Don't get discouraged. Someday when you go to the mailbox there will be little checks deposited there instead of the bills that you are now receiving.

It is better to laugh than to cry.

Dad's comment to us as we left home was simply, "Don't Forget Your Roots." It is agreed that he, the family, and the community gave us roots, we will remember and for which we always will be thankful.

Lessons learned while working with livestock: Walk slowly. Talk low. Be patient. Don't expect everything to go right. The animals are bigger than you. Respect them. You're smarter than they are but don't let them know it. Livestock may have had a bad day also. They are your bank account. Try to figure out what they will do next and what you will do next. Once things have gotten out of hand, give up.

There are people who sometimes ask what you would do if you were to return to your youth. The answer is simply, "Nothing different." We were always was quite content with what we had. There is little doubt that living in Eastern Montana developed a "can do" attitude that was vital to us in later years. Self-help books hadn't been written yet but the lessons that we learned on the prairie was seared into our very being. Help yourself was not only heard at the dining table but elsewhere at other times. Suppose we could have waited until those authors wrote their books telling of how to be successful but we just didn't have that luxury. We couldn't wait for their publications and, frankly, we didn't have money to buy books anyway.

I contend that it takes forty acres to raise a kid. A horse, a trusty dog and an angel or two provide other needed elements.

One thing that we all learned at an early age was not to hate or bear grudges. There were times, however, when we disagreed among ourselves but this attitude did not last long. We learned to get along with other people and not let our grudges go unresolved. It is difficult to fight with someone upon whom you would depend to provide help in your time of need. Cooperation and working together for everyone's benefit became a mantra for us all, kind of like the Three Musketeers and their philosophy of all for one and one for all.

I learned from experience that a person should dream of the future and do what is his heart's desire. Freedom to act and independence to get the job done is a Western ethic. Have a set of goals and carry through with them. But always remember to be flexible and be ready to make any needed corrections.

Oh, there were times in which disagreements took place in which problems arose within the family and in the community at large. Funny thing, though, these hassles did not last long. One moment there was fire and smoke and next there was reconciliation. No grudges or long-term revenge situations were evident. Get mad and get over it. On with the work at hand. No time for the luxury of conflict.

## HEALTH:

Dad was born in 1918. At the height of the worldwide Spanish Flu epidemic. He got sick and baby Stan was taken to a makeshift hospital in a two-story brick house in Wibaux known as the "Wagner Hospital." While there, Dad did not do well. In fact, assuming that he had died, medical personnel placed him in a cold upstairs room where they kept the bodies of those who had died during this devastating epidemic. Miraculously the cold air revived Dad and as he lay there he began to cry. A nurse walked by the room, heard a noise, investigated and there she found the baby alive. After the care that was made available in that quite primitive facility he recovered and grew up to be a healthy cowboy. Legend has it that as Dad was suffering heart disease in his later years and as he was nearing death's door again, this same nurse visited him and they spent considerable time together one afternoon at home in Wibaux. The part of this story concerning the nurse's final visit is my recollection from discussions with Dad and is subject to controversy as no other relative can verify it. If there are readers who can confirm this visitation, please contact the author. Until that day, the story will stand as is written here.

Being sick in those days was no treat. Earache seemed to be one of my maladies. Warm goose grease poured into fevered ears provided a wonderful relief. I would not recommend this treatment today, as I believe that there are now penicillin or antibiotics that would be a more approved method to handle the condition. Access to healthcare was always a factor. Quality of care was also questionable as there were no extensive medications, equipment or advanced medical knowledge in those days. We had a doctor in town. He came to Wibaux after graduating from the Creighton Medical School in Omaha. His medical office was set up in a two-story frame house in the town's Davis Addition. To my way of thinking it was a bit of a sinister place for some reason or another. Doctors or hospitals did not rank high in a kid's list of special places. Old Doc would complete the required physical examination of athletes before high school football practice and as needed during the year. There was one other time he was called on by the family when as a child I fell out of the parked pickup truck in front of Helviks Grocery hitting my head on the concrete curb knocking me senseless. The good doctor told my folks at that time that I would have trouble the rest of my life because of that incident. He was correct as it probably resulted in my latent epilepsy, which developed years later. Thankfully this malady is controlled now but it played a major part in my life. It became a point of discrimination and a limitation for me during those early formative years.

In those days there were precious few effective products to treat wounds or sickness. I remember in addition to warm goose grease in the ear, Absorbine Junior and horse liniment, aspirin, Bactine, iodine, mercurochrome, bandages, calamine lotion, tape and gauze, burn ointment, Vick's Vapor Rub, eye drops and cod liver oil were the most common remedies. If those weren't effective, then bed rest, fluids, and time healed all wounds. Bag Balm was a good ointment for use on chapped hands. Its green metal container could be found on a shelf in the barn. Aspirin was always around. A big bottle usually was sitting on the windowsill or on the orange crate "table in the bunkhouse. One of the "miracle drugs" that came onto the scene was sulfa drug, which the pharmacist would package in little paper packets. Packets were torn open, and the loose yellowish powder was spread unto an open wound. This readily aided healing. Horse liniment for aches and pains, and disinfectants could be found either in the kitchen or the shop. Band-Aids and bandages were always around for use on cuts, scrapes and abrasions.

Great Grandma Josie Trollope, J.E. Trollope's wife, was a midwife and in that capacity she delivered, I am told many babies in Wibaux.

Growing up on a Montana ranch/farm was about the best experience that a kid could have. But there were times that weren't quite as fun as others. I remember one time while walking through the woods I encountered a porcupine. These elusive creatures caused some problems with livestock. I decided to attack this critter with a stick to save possible injury to cattle and horses in the pasture. Hitting a porcupine with a stick is a futile endeavor because the animal is quite indestructible. Their bodies are covered with quills, which can be dislodged into your own hide if care is not taken. Fortunately, I was left quill-free and unscathed. After this event, though, I noticed that my right thumb hurt. I expect the stick caused the injury as it twisted in my hand causing a bruised bone. Some time after that I was taken to the NPBA (Northern Pacific Beneficial Association Hospital) where an X-ray or fluoroscope revealed deterioration on the right thumb bone. It turned out to be osteomyelitis. The surgeon opened it up and scrapped the bone to remove a staph infection. To this day, my right thumb has a surgical scar. I spent a few days in the hospital and soon returned to the activities of being a 10-year-old farm boy. Decades later it was reported to me by medical personnel that this staph like infection could well have been fatal. Such was medical care in 1950, in this case very effective.

One other serious injury occurred while riding my bicycle at Grandma Stockwell's home. We would ride down the hill as fast as we could and fly through a dust accumulation in the road. When I hit this loose dirt, the bike went end over end and I was knocked unconscious for a period of time. After a bit, I regained consciousness and there did not appear to be any complications. Although it may have been a factor in my contracting epilepsy while in my teens. Head trauma now is recognized as a serious event. In those days, it was just an inconvenience. Being kicked in the head by an animal, thrown from a horse, or hit on the head during construction was taken lightly.

Riding horses and bucking steers is a dangerous activity. One evening, Dude T. was riding an unruly critter as we spectators cheered. Unfortunately, the animal's head jerked up with its horn catching Dude on the right cheekbone. He wore a red scar there for the rest of his life.

Sickness occurred frequently in our family of three brothers and our sister. Measles both Red & German variety, chicken pox, mumps, colds, ear aches, the "itch" and other childhood diseases never passed our door without making a stop or two. In those days, it was just a fact of life that you would succumb to these maladies as a part of growing up. Disease and misfortune almost became a right of passage, it seemed.

Going to the doctor was not the highlight of our week. As a little kid, the folks took my brothers and me to the Glendive Hospital for shots. One by one we were led into the examining room for the inoculations. Loud noises and crying could be heard emanating from that mysterious room next door. I was the last to go in. The nurse found me hiding behind a door. She peeked through the crack in the door and reached out to grab me and I recall kicking her in the shins. This resulted in being handled none too lightly and after that came the shot.

One other time, I got impetigo infection under my toenails necessitating removal of a couple of toenails by the doctor. Sometimes I seem to remember yet today the pain that was associated with this procedure especially when my feet get cold. The brightly lighted examining room, white sheets, and medical personnel made a big impression on us kids whenever we were taken to the hospital. Scary!!!

Epilepsy restricted many of the activities that I would have participated in during school. The perceived danger of seizures held me back from some activities and may have caused me some adjustment problems. Even though my attacks were infrequent-every seven months like clockwork—until I got the correct medication my wings were "clipped." After receiving the correct medication there were no more incidents as long as the prescribed medicines were taken regularly. The malady was greatly misunderstood in those days. My epilepsy was a subject of hushed conversation by relatives who showed concern over my health. Today we know epilepsy is just one of a large number of neurological conditions that can be traced to abnormalities in the brain and nervous system and that in many or most cases medication or surgical procedures can correct. Insanity, demonic, moronic, or mental handicaps were erroneously attributed to seizure activity. Sadly, these misconceptions persisted long after the witch-hunts were explained.

## NATIVE AMERICANS:

While working the farm field on top of the hill south of our homestead house Dad found a very small white arrowhead, which he thought could have been used in Native American ceremonies. It was thought that the hill might have been a meeting place for powwows. This never was verified and probably is not true. But it shows that the farmers were cognizant of others who had lived on the land before them. The newcomers showed the same respect for the land that the early inhabitants had. Theirs was a search for a connection with these early peoples in an attempt to understand their culture and in appreciation for what they also had to endure on the plains of Montana.

Granddad would tell stories of Wisconsin's early days; in the late 1800's and early 1900's. Roaming Natives seeking a campsite would stop at their farm home. They were given permission time after time. But some problems did arise, it appears. Not certain if it involved loss of chickens from the chicken house or corn from the field. At any rate, young Dan was home as the tribe came to the door asking for campsite use. He told them that they were no longer welcome to camp on their farmland because of the difficulties that they experienced in the previous year. The group's spokesperson said, "Oh, you mean John. He is not with us. The big man upstairs took him away. He steal 'em too much." Permission denied.

Another time Natives were camped on the farm in Wisconsin and an altercation developed. It seems that one of Dan's brothers, probably Len, was wrestling one of them inside a tent when a head was outlined in the tent's fabric. Another Native picked up a club and was about to strike this protruding head but was stopped by one of the boys. This probably saved someone at least a monumental headache.

Granddad told of the baseball games the locals would engage in with the Natives. Sitting in the stands with the score always very lopsided to the advantage of the Native peoples their chief kept saying, "No Fun, No Fun."

## OIL:

One day during the early the oil boom of the 1950's there were seismographing operations all over our farm. The workers were called "roughnecks." They busied themselves drilling holes and dynamiting for seismic wave evaluation in the hopes of finding black gold. One crew set up shop behind our house, drilled eleven holes, packing them with explosives, detonating them in pairs of two holes at a time with the hope of finding oil sign on their electronic equipment. The holes were filled with water to increase the accuracy of the seismic picture. When the blast went off; dirt, mud, and water were blown high in the air. Other than waking up every critter in the valley and muddying up the sod nothing productive was accomplished.

During an especially severe dry spell, an oil company geologist had set up a device in the middle of our road. He peered into the device for what seemed to be hours. Dad afar off was observing this activity and finally curiosity got the better of him. He approached the geologist with the question, "Can't you see that the ground is dry without that machine?" I expect that there was a chuckle or two resulting in a discussion as to what was being found. Needless to say no oil wells were drilled. No oil was discovered and no money was received. But there was a shared hopeful observation of better days ahead. For at least now it had been determined that the earth below was probably as dry as the earth above.

## PRACTICAL JOKES:

One hot day, while working on the farm with some friends, Dad went to town for equipment repair parts. As he was leaving, his friend asked that he stop by the JC Penney store in Beach to buy him a new work shirt. Dad picked up the new shirt, unwrapped it and substituted for it a ragged shirt that had been worn while dehorning cattle. This old buttonless shirt was covered with blood and sweat. He delivered the shirt to the cowboy who could not believe his eyes as he unwrapped the package. A loud protest was heard and the hired hand promptly made plans to make a call on that JC Penney store being fired up with his complaint. All the while the rest of the hands had a good laugh.

Dan and some of his contemporaries used to operate a coalmine in the Yates, Montana area. This must have been quite an operation as they had some employees and were engaged in local coal delivery operations. Practical jokes were the order of the day. They usually revolved around requests for items the miners needed to be picked up in town by the wagon masters hauling coal to the market in Beach. On one occasion, one of the miners asked for a pint of stove paint to be used on his wood-burning stove. Well, the can was opened and the paint was replaced with used oil. The miner painted his stove with this oil leaving a beautiful black coating on the unit. This sheen persisted until the stove was fired up with wood. The oil began to smoke as the heat evaporated the "paint." The good intentions of home improvement went up in smoke!

Another time, a miner asked for a ten-pound bag of sugar. The bag was emptied and its contents replaced with salt. The miner's wife began to cook a prune sauce using the bag's "sugar." Of course, the finished product was inedible being permeated with salt. The miner went to the grocery store and complained vehemently. A bag of sugar was obtained in exchange. But the real "kicker" was that the grocer had just received a very large amount of sugar in that shipment and to be certain that there was no more difficulty, each bag was opened and tested for salt.

Granddad would tell these and other stories to us grandchildren as he rocked in that old leather chair. He laughed so hard that tears would come to his eyes.

One practical joke that was played on our Luther League group was an unusually humorous event. We car-pooled to visit a Luther League youth group in a nearby small Montana town. The ride was long. When we got there everyone wanted to go to the restroom. The host group had placed a "Restroom" sign on the boiler room door. Upon entering there were no facilities other than an old steam boiler and the attending shop. All of the local youth's attention was riveted on that door as the new comers entered. Of course, everybody laughed when we went in, turned around and walked back red faced. The toilet we were informed of later was in the little wooden house behind the church!!

## SUCCESS:

Dude tells of a story that Dad had told him about one of his early successes. He and another cowboy had gone to the Dickinson Sales Barn to sell some cattle. While there, Dad's cows were not sold in the morning. He was informed that hogs were scheduled to be sold ahead of Dad's cattle in the afternoon. This meant that all of the cattle buyers would leave for lunch; probably not return to the sales barn and this would result in fewer bidders for his livestock. The auctioneer ran the hogs into the ring ahead of the cows seeing the possible problem standing in his way of getting a good price for his livestock, Dad bought all the hogs in a short time. His livestock was then run into the sales ring and were sold at a good price before lunch. His buddy asked what they were going to do with all of those hogs since Dad didn't have any feed for them. Being practical they figured that they would cross that bridge when they came to it. The hogs were loaded both cowboys knowing full well that they were not experts in raising hogs and that there were scarce means of taking care of them. The porkers were taken out to the ranch where they were turned loose in the pasture. That fall they rounded up the wild pigs that had multiplied and they were sold for a considerable sum of money, much to everyone's surprise and delight. Free range hogs. A new concept!

# TECHNOLOGY:

A traveling salesman from Denver came to the house to sell Dad an arc welder now that we had gotten electricity. This eager salesman arrived before Dad returned from the field. While waiting around, the salesman asked us three boys if we had ever seen a German Lugar 9mm pistol. Of course we hadn't. Subsequently he pulled this large gun out from under the car seat and told us to look over across the creek to a large sand rock, which was about the size of a small truck. He shot several times and the bullets ricocheted off into space. The loud noise and excitement we'd never forget. It did cause quite a stir to mom who was in the kitchen, though.

Dad finally met with the salesman after approaching the farmyard riding on his IHC Model M tractor and they went into the house to talk about the value of having a welder on the farm. It was agreed that this was something that was needed even though $400 seemed a high price to pay. They finally made a deal and the papers were signed. Sitting around drinking coffee afterwards, the salesman remarked that Dad sure was easy to deal with and wasn't as nasty as our neighbor who was located a mile or so away. Dad said that neighbor was his uncle. Salesman said not the house by the red scoria hill, but down the lane from the Cottonwood Community Hall. Dad said that was his other uncle. Salesman said not by the lane but the farm located on the west fork of the road two miles away. Dad said that this was his father-in-law. Salesman said that he was mistaken and said that it was straight away on the east fork of the road. Dad said that that was his father's place. Well, the salesman gave up after that finished his coffee and we all had a good laugh. The welder was delivered in a few weeks and it became one of the best investments we ever made. It sat in the shop for so many years. It was difficult to see it go at auction after Dad died.

After getting the welder, it was decided to cut the fenders and body off of a 1939 Dodge auto we had bought in town. In its stripped down form it was later christened "77-D." Dad wanted to make it into a "bug" to use traveling to the pasture to look after the sheep and cattle. We all watched with great interest as this cutting tool blazed away, sparks flying everywhere. What fun we were having. That night, however, all three of us boys woke up crying out that we were all blind. Dad jumped out of bed and began reading the welder User's Manual in a frenzy. He finally came across a warning that stated that the welding arc was not to be watched as it would "sun burn" our eyes. If this happened, I believe it stated, we were to put raw potatoes on our eyes. Needless to say that our eyesight returned the next morning but we never looked at the welding arc flash again. Probably one of the most valuable safety lessons learned on the farm that summer.

Lawrence and Ardys would have us over for Thanksgiving and also sometimes at Christmas. Uncle Lawrence got a new TV set in 1954. They were some of the first in our area to have this new invention. I especially remember the live special report one night, which showed the Russian military running their tanks down the Budapest, Hungary streets in the midst of the Hungarian Revolt. Staring at that black and white set was a wonder. We could hardly comprehend what was transpiring. Imagine the world coming directly into the living room. These were shades of things to come. On rooftops or on metal towers the required TV antennae began sprouting up all over. Antennae had to be pointed directly towards the broadcasting station. Reception was always a point of discussion. Two major stations existed for us. Channel 2 Dickinson & Channel 8 Williston. Sometimes, "skipped signals" would be picked up allowing for stations in Fargo or even from cities farther out to be received. Everyone would try their best to purchase and install better and improved antennae bragging of the programs from far away places they had received. In about 1940 the encyclopedia featured an article about the future of TV. It stated that it was a good invention but that it would not be feasible to broadcast on a large national scale because of the need to have a booster broadcasting station every 25 miles. In 1954, this encyclopedia article could be believable. But now satellite TV, anyone?

I remember when television first came to Wibaux. Not many could afford to buy this new almost magical device. There were only a few houses that featured large aluminum antennae giving witness to their progressive, if not wealthy, life style. Our house did not have a TV set until about 1956 or so. It was a small 15-inch Admiral portable that received only about one channel regularly and maybe two or three depending on the atmospheric conditions. A black and white picture punctuated with heavy "snow" was the quality of our reception. We learned to look at the screen through "half closed eyes" in order to improve the broadcast image. Jack's Radio & TV shop downtown got a few old TV's in his inventory. Jack had installed one unit up in the storefront window for passersby to see. A speaker was mounted outside so we could hear the news program, "Douglas Edwards & The News." I used to sit on my bicycle seat on the sidewalk outside and marvel at those pictures and sounds.

One early innovation was to attach a clear plastic sheet over the TV screen. This would provide for "color" reception. The top of the plastic sheet was blue (sky), the middle color was a pinkish color (face color) and the third level was green (ground level).

## SHEEP STORIES:

We took the "Bug 77-D", automobile, amid a cloud of blue oil smoke down to the pasture to check on Granddad's sheep. Located about in the middle of the section was a large windmill adjacent was a huge wooden stock water tank from which the sheep could drink. When we got there, we saw the calamity that had occurred. Somehow, the sheep had been crowded into the tank. The ones in the back pushed the others into the tank until the tank was filled with floating dead animals. Their wool had become saturated and about twenty of them drowned. There went the profits. It was a difficult job to haul fat, wet, dead sheep from that tank. Thankfully, the hired help was charged with that duty.

Granddad's sheep stories could fill a large portion of this book if written in detail. One other distressing event that took place was the time that the sheep were sheared too early in the spring and a cold, wet snow came chilling the naked sheep. It is not known how many died from pneumonia or exposure but it was more than a few. As I recall they took refuge from the wind jam-packing themselves into the buffalo berry bushes where they died.

One other time, there had been no rain for months and the dams that provided water for the sheep had receding shorelines leaving a muddy expanse before the water could be reached. The sheep would venture out into the mud and become stuck. Grandson Gordy Ueckert would go out into the mud, fasten a lariat around the sheep and Granddad Trollope would pull them from the mud using a pick up truck. More than one way to herd sheep.

As kids we enrolled in 4-H and got into the sheep business. We had some very fine Columbia animals having good quality wool rich in lanolin. The wool brought about fifty cents per pound with each fleece being about fourteen pounds. The old ewes raised hefty slaughter lambs for sale also. They brought about $20 each on the fat lamb market. Among the challenges of raising sheep was the ram that shared the pen with the ewes. He had massive horns and an ill temper. He would run up behind you and would butt you. This was a serious situation, as he would continue attacking until you removed yourself from his territory. One time our hired hand was confronted by this cantankerous bully. He picked up a club and began to retaliate. He was not too successful as he continued to hit the ram on the horns seemingly to no avail. His thick wool coat cushioned the impact of the club and he showed no response for the beating. The attack finally subsided and each retreated to his own territory. The ram to the feed bunk and the hired man to an area beyond the fence. Then one day this abusive bully was loaded up in the truck for a tour of the elsewhere. We were all glad to see that ram peering out of slit in the truck's tailgate as he was headed off to market to where we knew was a better place. At least it was a better place for us if not him!

One old adage said that when the price of wool was high, we would soon go to war. Possibly, the rationale was that the demand for the fiber increased due to its use for blankets and uniforms.

Sheep shearing time was not one of our favorites on the ranch. It did allow for a team approach, however, as everyone was needed to gather, pen, and work the animals onto the wooden shearing platform where the itinerant sheep shearer would shear a sheep for about thirty cents each, as I recall. It would only take a short time for a good shearer to do his work. As the shearing began, the first sheep were fitted with a fine coiffure. However, as the day and the whiskey bottle wore on, more and more sheep were sporting red marks from the sharp shears. The fleece was tied into a bundle using a fiber string. The bundle then was tossed up into the waiting woolsack, which had been soaked in the horse tank and stretched on an eight-foot high tripod. Inside the sack one of us kids would tamp the fleeces tight. The tied fleece bundles were pitched overhead into the sack and along with the fleece came manure, dust, grease, and sheep ticks, all of which landed in our hair and caked on our T-shirts. The bag was about eight feet long and would hold about 300 pounds. When full, a large needle was used to stitch the opening shut. Raising sheep became a moneymaker for Granddad Trollope and others in the family. They would buy "gummer" sheep for about twenty dollars per head. These old sheep had few teeth and were skin and bones; hence, the term "gummer" became their label. Some died in the winter but a respectable number lived on to have single or twin lambs in the spring. These lambs would grow and in the fall they would be sheared yielding six to eight pound fleeces worth fifty cents per pound and the lambs were sold at auction as slaughter or feeder lambs at a price of about twenty dollars per each. The old "gummer" sheep would only shear out at about six pounds each.

Lambs and ewe sheep were easy to care for. However, "Bum lambs", those whose mothers had died or who were not claimed by the mother ewe, had to be fed manually with skim milk served up in Coca Cola bottles fitted with rubber nipples. The lambs did quite well on this fare of cow's milk. Their joyful enthusiasm to be fed was something to behold. These little critters would run, jump and cavort about carrying on antics that were better than any circus entertainment. Many of the bum lambs were obtained free from large sheep ranchers whose ranches were located about six miles north of our place.

Sheep were "branded" by using a paintbrush and paint insignia on their backs. A few had had ear tags but mostly red or black paint on their backs would designate ownership.

The sheep that we raised were Rambouillet, black face or Columbia breeds.

## TOUGH TIMES:

During the tough times of the 1930's-1940's survival was a challenge. To raise a crop, feed animals, and to maintain the household was everyone's job. Stories are told of Grandma Mabel Stockwell's efforts in earning money. She would go to town to buy flour and sugar to bring back home to make doughnuts that were taken to town and sold. The money received was used to buy more flour and sugar to take home to make doughnuts to take to town to sell so that more flour and sugar could be purchased. The story has no ending. It showed her perseverance that was mirrored throughout her whole life. Never give up.

Tough times were frequent. The crops were constantly being evaluated. Comparing fields and walking in fields was a constant activity. In bad years we could sometimes count the few stalks of the grain standing to greet us. Topics of conversation with neighbors constantly centered on how healthy the crops were, how much rain had fallen, whether any hail damage occurred, grass hopper infestations, costs, and grain prices.

I remember one time when a car salesman came out to the ranch and he convinced the folks to buy a new Chevrolet sedan. The expected harvest must have allowed for this decision to take place even though all night long the family did not sleep well and considerations were weighed as to whether we should return the blue and white, four door auto that was left sitting out in the yard. We literally did not sleep well on this decision. Must have been sold on the "Lay Awake Plan!"

As we would drive by and walk in he wheat fields that were so carefully planted, we could sometimes count the puny stand of growing grain. The seed heads sometimes were filled only with a few shriveled seeds due to the excessive heat and drought during their formation in the months of June and July. Between the sparse stalks of grain grew the hated weeds. Canadian and Russian thistles seemed to grow every dry year. These weeds would have to be harvested as a hay crop to feed the cattle that would be our only cash crop in those years when the grain harvest dwindled. Cattle provided collateral for our outstanding loans, which needed to be renewed for next year's farm operating costs and to provide for the winter months. Field corn that was planted would only grow to a height of about five feet on the hills but taller in the watered low spots of the field. Corn gave us a fine meal of roasting ears when slathered with homemade butter and those new crop potatoes tasted marvelously when served with new peas in a cream sauce. We never knew that there was a difference between eating common field corn and that fancy sweet corn we found available in later years. Digging potatoes was a real chore. It involved wrestling the small red potatoes from the dry hardened soil. Potatoes piled high in the root cellar represented our family's food against the cold winter winds that we knew would soon visit us. We were lucky to have that potato supply, our own chicken eggs, and a cow to provide milk. There were times when we would butcher a hog and there was sometimes venison game hanging in the grain bin that could be counted on to serve up a meal for us. When an old hen ceased laying eggs she ended up in a pot of noodles or dumplings.

Tough economic times were caused by poor quality and disappointing crop yields. The value of the crops of wheat, hay, barley, and oats and the price of cattle decreased. There was no hay or grain to feed the animals during those times. Canadian thistle weeds, sunflowers, Russian thistles, and any other green plant was cut and piled in haystacks for livestock feed during the coming winter. What it took for survival during these drought years is almost incomprehensible now days.

I can remember:
5-cent candy bars, 10-cent comic books, 10-cent Cokes, 75-cent haircut, 3-cent letter postage, 1-cent "penny postcards", "Air Mail" stamps, $1,200 per year tuition at Concordia College, Cars costing $1.00 per pound, 85 cents per hour wages at the college cafeteria

$1.85 per hour with time and a half for over 40 hours being employed in oil field construction work. We worked 70 hours per week and were required to drive or ride about100 miles round trip each day—much of it in the back of a pick up truck.

We rented a farm in Wibaux for $20.00 per month. (4 acres, barn, chicken house, garage, root cellar, water well, and outhouse.) This is where we wintered during the school year.

Thirty cent gasoline.

The price list goes on and on . . .

# FIRES:

Dad would take a fruit jar containing drinking water to the field. This old fruit jar was securely wrapped in wet burlap sack and tied with sisal twine. It was placed in the toolbox for fieldwork. On one occasion the water jar fell to the ground or was left sitting out in the sun. The refraction of the sunlight on the water and glass evidently ignited a prairie fire. Prairie fires created much excitement in the community.

The Blue Mountain Telephone Company party line was our communication with the whole Cottonwood Community. When the phone rang, two longs and two shorts at our house, we would answer along with everyone else on the line. "Rubbering" or listening in on everybody's conversations on the party line was a pastime. This proved to be bothersome outside of the times when an emergency message was to be sent to everyone on the line. Prairie fire was one of those times. Looking to the north on one occasion we could see smoke just this side of Blue Mountain and the fire was moving quite rapidly. Farmers were rousted out. Riding their tractors pulling farm implements to be used in controlling the blaze began traveling to the fire. Others would have fire dampers-fire beaters composed of a pitchfork handle attached to a heavy rubber material. These rather crude tools were used to literally beat out the fire. Lightning caused most fires but there could be some fires caused by intentional burning of stubble and roadside weeds or possibly equipment's hot exhaust pipes. Each township had a Fire Warden whose job it was to issue burning permits or advise of burning regulations and to be engaged in fire prevention.

# CATTLE STORIES:

There never was a great distinction between sheepherders and cattle ranchers. We had both animals on our farm. There never was a range war over sheep or cattle as we saw in old movies. There was one small confrontation, I believe, between a sheepherder and a cattleman. This was settled by double fencing at least one pasture. Two fences were separated by only about eight inches. This solved the livestock fence crawling problem. In the end, the cattleman began raising sheep also. In fact, it took both sheep and cattle to assure some sort of income in ranching operations because wheat, oats, barley, and the sometimes corn crop could not provide for our needs during drought years. Chickens and turkeys also were our mainstays providing eggs & meat for the table and for sale in town.

When we had cattle on the farm they numbered about eighty head plus about seven milk cows. The milk cows furnished about enough cream weekly to fill a five-gallon can, which was hauled to the railroad depot in Wibaux where a wire tag was affixed to the can listing either the Dickinson, ND or Bismarck, ND creamery as its destination. We would receive a check in the amount of about eight dollars for this cream. Take note that there was no refrigeration at the depot or at our ranch so this cream would accumulate over several days being exposed summer heat. What kept the contents from spoiling is a mystery to this day. There was one occasion, however, when the cream can overturned in our car's trunk spilling its contents. Its ghastly odor never left the vehicle. Don't cry over spilt milk but spilt cream is a bane forever.

I can still hear the sound of empty cream cans being tossed and rolled about at the railroad depot. The locomotive's hiss, belching steam and coal cinders along with the engine's whistles and bells will be forever a memory. The plank decking adjacent to the depot served as a platform for the REA iron wheeled green wagon hauling cream cans, freight and luggage. The clanking sound of the load as the iron wheels creaked along the platform is gone forever.

Milk cows were bothered with flies in the summer. Seeking relief they would swat flies with their tails sometimes hitting you in the face while milking. A new wonderful pesticide came upon the market and could be purchased cheaply at the store in town. Its name was DDT. When this miracle powder was sprinkled onto the backs of the milk cows flies rolled off to the straw floor below or into the milk pail whichever was closer. Accumulated chicken mites also boiled out and rolled out of crevices in the milking stanchions when this powder was sprinkled on them. Sometimes these mites accumulated to a depth of about one inch. DDT was a wonder pesticide on the farm. Two other "wonder" drug type chemicals came to assist in the production of potatoes and beef. Paris Green (arsenic) powder was added to a bucket of water and this liquid was sprinkled on growing potato plants to kill potato bugs. When exposed to the chemical these fleshy bugs dropped off onto the hot, dry soil below. The other chemical was a creosote type of liquid disinfectant that was mixed with water and was doused onto sores caused during the castration of bulls at branding time. It is a wonder that we survived all of these latest innovations that in today's literature tell us that these are all hazardous chemicals. Another very effective remedy bought from the drug store included pure nicotine for treatment of turkey mites. Nicotine was placed on the wings of the turkeys ridding those birds free of those pesky mites.

Gathering milk cows for milking at evening time was a chore. We would sometimes ride our bicycles out to the pasture for this roundup. On the way back to the barn the cattle would form a single line and would trudge down the rutted path leading to the home place at sundown. Sometimes this trek was made easier for us while riding our bicycles being pulled along by the cow's tail.

Living in Wibaux during the school year we rented a small farm having a barn housing one milk cow and a chicken house with about two dozen hens that supplied eggs. An occasional fat hen from this flock was drafted to provide us with meat for our chicken and dumplings Sunday dinner. Our animals had to be fed and watered. It was an easy chore to feed and water the chickens. All that we had to do is to pump water from the well, carry it to the chicken house and scoop out some feed from a barrel. Chicken house water pans and feed containers sitting on the ground were filled. Accumulated ice from yesterday's watering had to be disposed of and the fresh water was splashed in. Feed was primarily oats with maybe some wheat and weed screening from the grain elevator. Chickens also were fed oyster shells to provide calcium needed for sturdy eggshells. Feeding and watering the milk cow was a task that required hard work and skill. The cow was tethered in the barn and a fork full of hay had to be placed in the manger. Watering the cow meant untying the animal and leading her down to Beaver Creek where she probably lapped up five or ten gallons of the clear flowing water stream. One time the milk cow broke loose running a couple of miles away being chased by yours truly. Mom rushed to the car and joined in the chase, ending near the city dump with the capture of the wayward Guernsey. The weather was cool but all participants were hot and sweaty following this fiasco. You can bet that the hills still echo from the curses, cries, and bellowing from that episode.

One hot summer day we went out to bring in the milk cows for milking and along the way one of the large cows up and died. Evidently, she must have gotten into some toxic weeds and it proved fatal to this critter. It was decided to skin the cow, salt down the hide and sell it to the scrap dealer in Beach, ND. Skinning a cow during the heat of summer, using poor knives, and declining light conditions nearing sundown proved to be an unpleasant task. A cowhide is several inches thick and when folded up and tied weighs a considerable amount. Tugging, pulling, and lifting this hide into the truck was a job. It seems like we might have gotten seven dollars for our efforts. Never sought a repeat of this money making project. Some would say that there are more ways to skin a cat. There is only one way to skin a cow, hard work.

Stock cows were a different exposure. They relied upon us to feed them bales of hay in the corral behind the barn. We would harvest upwards of 80 ton of forage each summer for this purpose. Sometimes the hay was good prairie grass of blue stem, red grass, brome, crested wheat, buffalo grass and alfalfa in the good years when rain was plentiful. Russian thistles, Canadian thistles, straw, pigweed, wild oats, and a variety of other weeds provided the winter fare for the cattle when the summer was extremely dry and the growth of good hay was not possible. Good hay was like money in the bank. Livestock owners learned early that as long as a cow had some sort of wind shelter and water with the roughage, they could survive subzero temperatures just fine. There were some occasions when we would feed sparingly expensive cottonseed cake as a protein supplement. The only breed of cattle that was popular in those days were the white faced red Herefords as they proved to be hardy enough to endure the Montana environs. Oh, there were times when an old milk cow's Jersey, Holstein, or Guernsey progeny would be mixed with the bunch. These pretty much were the first to go to market in the fall of the year. Mostly, we tried to sell our 500-700 pound feeder calves around Thanksgiving time. Selling the calves at that time of the year saved on hay because we didn't have to feed them during the winter months and those calves were about the heaviest at that time having gained about all the weight they could having only prairie grass for feed. These feeders were then sold to buyers who plied them with corn to produce the finest marbled beef in the world. Connoisseurs of beef slaughtered for skillets soon learn that grass fed beef tends to be tough, as does milk cow meat.

## BRANDING:

In the spring of the year livestock branding, dehorning, vaccinating and castration of the calves was conducted on every ranch. Branding calves became a community activity that brought everyone together. Ranch hands from the community would gather to help out. Cowboys would bring their trusty steeds to round up the cattle and herd them into pens at the corral. Calves were separated from the cows, as they were the guests of honor in this branding activity. Gathering up the cattle, herding them into corrals, and setting up for the grand affair took most of the morning. Branding irons were assembled. The fire was stoked using scrap lumber and a few dead tree limbs found in the pasture's sparse timber. Disinfectant was mixed up using a batch of creosote, dehorning blood stop powder brought out, vaccine and hypodermic needles were placed out of the way high atop a fence post. When preparations were completed the work began. One by one the critters were brought out or were lassoed, bulldogged, picked up and laid down where they were castrated, vaccinated, dehorned, and branded. The smaller calves weighing around one hundred or so pounds were caught with a rope and a cowboy would approach the animal grabbing it by the legs and upending the calf throwing him to the ground. One cowboy would sit on his neck while a second cowboy held down the back legs as the red-hot iron was applied to the critter's rump leaving a clearly defined stamp in place of the winter hair. A hissing sound of seared skin, and burning hair could be heard and smelled. The smaller animal's horns were treated with dehorning paste or their nubs pinched off their heads using dehorning tools. All the while this activity was taking place the calf's mother would bawl out responding to the cry of their calves being worked on. The bull calves had to be castrated where they lay. When their "seeds" were removed the incision was doused with disinfectant. The larger animals were branded and serviced using a homemade cattle chute. Cattle were urged through the chute and their head and necks were trapped, the rear end of the animal was blocked using a cedar post so that he could not back out of the chute. They were trapped and immobile. Horns were lopped off using a dehorning tool. This was painful to the animal and resulted in an animal recoiling, jumping and expelling a bellowing roar. Blood spurted high into the air from the wound. Blood stop powder was applied to assist in clotting. The whole scene was one of major chaos with bellowing calves, mooing cows, yelling and cussing cowboys, neighing of horses, stamping of feet, noise from fence wire being tested by enclosed cows, dust in the air, steers jumping over tall fences, and dogs running around tasting the remains of the surgery. There were times when unruly steers knocked over the branding iron forge scattering irons and red-hot coals around the scene. This brought more yelling and cussing from the cowboys adding to the din of the moment. Smoke billowed above the whole affair while the rancher mentally counted the critter as another "mortgage lifter". These animals were sold in the fall of the year when they reached about 600 pounds bringing about 65-75 cents per pound. The money received at the auction sales barn brought income that was used to pay off the bank's loan, hence the term, "mortgage lifter." When branding was complete, the irons were cooled in a bucket of water with attendant cloud of steam and then stored beneath the shop to await next year. Following the morning's work all hands deferred to the ranch house where feasting prevailed. Loud laughter and bravado were the topics during these joyous times.

## STORMS:

Snow storms, windstorms, dust storms, rainstorms, and hail storms were always a part of growing up on the ranch. Without today's scientific methods of meteorology and storm forecasting, people were left to watching the sky with the hopes that they could determine weather patterns. Large, black thunderheads with rapid decreases in temperature amid a greenish cast on the horizon certainly meant tornadoes could be expected. Sometimes heavy, humid conditions that were experienced gave some warning of the mighty winds that sometimes rapidly developed.

The winter season brought the necessity for increased observation of the skies. "Sundogs", a halo surrounding the sun, supposedly gave indication that tomorrow was going to be cold. Later on we found this was due to the sun reflecting off ice crystals in the sky. Of course, during these times the weather was already cold so this predictor of things to come became somewhat worthless or at least redundant. Cold is cold with or without "Sundogs."

Red skies at sundown meant something also, don't know what it was, though. Had something to do with "Red Sky At Night, Sailor's Delight." Never could see the benefit of this predictor because we didn't have any sailors or bodies of water around Wibaux County. We did have a healthy respect for the weather and the damage it could wreak, however.

One day in May, my brothers and a friend or two were down on Beaver Creek climbing the bluffs, throwing rocks into the water and running through the trees as we were wont to do whenever we got the chance. A heavy rainstorm resulting in a tornado came up suddenly and we all decided to run for the shelter of a vacant farmstead about a quarter of a mile distant. Upon arriving I suggested that we take refuge in the chicken house but was outvoted by the others who wanted to go into the barn which was located only about four feet away. While taking refuge in the barn a mighty wind erupted. We watched as a trailer was toppled and rolled into and destroying the outhouse some forty feet away. The barn rose up from its foundation several inches and dust flew everywhere. Others in the group reported hearing a freight train-like sound. Me, I didn't hear a thing. When everything settled down we stepped outside and we were horrified to find that the chicken house had been blown away and lay smashed against a nearby hillside. Electric power lines were lying on the ground in the yard. Soaking wet we all marched back the Peterson home in town where the folks were attending a meeting of the Cottonwood Homemakers Club. We had more of an adventure that day then we had counted on. Someone said that I said a short prayer during this affair. It was simply, "O God, Not Now." I cannot remember this response to the tornado. We all were caught up in the chaos taking place.

A year or two before, we had a similar event that took place on the ranch, some twelve miles north of Wibaux. My brothers and I always were outside running about and exploring. On some occasions, a rainstorm would come up and we would spend the time in the small pump house building near the well. It was a joy to hear the rain on the roof and to see water running down the yard. On this occasion, the wind came up, the sky darkened and Mom yelled for us to head for the house. We put up a little argument, but decided to do as she had requested and that we'd better head for the house. We had not been in the house but a short time when a wind rose up and we watched as the pump house being lifted straight up thirty feet into the air, tumbled over the REA electric lines, and smashed into a large haystack near the barn. Dad came home at about that time and was unable to get out of his truck due to the air pressure created by the high winds. The electric cables broke and a loose line was causing electrical arcing as it hit the ground near the truck close by the house where we were. Again, we were so blessed to escape without injury!

Lightning has had a tendency to strike John Trollope's homestead. One time during breakfast a bolt of lightning came into the kitchen window, stripped Alberta of her clothes, flashed into the basement, broke John's nose, returning upstairs where it exited out of the same window! For the rest of John's life he shook and shivered whenever a dark cloud appeared in the sky.

Ranchers were always looking to the skies not only for storms but also for the rain that we prayed for. Without rain dry land farming took on a new definition. Rainfall in our part of Eastern Montana is normally only about 12-15 inches per year. Some years there was little or no rain and as a result wheat, barley, and oat crops were not worth harvesting. This is one of the saddest of all our experiences. We needed feed for our cattle, sheep, and horses so we would go out and mow for hay Canadian thistles, sunflowers, and weeds of all descriptions in the fields. This forage would be bunched together in windrows and would eventually have to be hauled to the hay corral in a 1937 Chevrolet truck or hayrack pulled by the "M" tractor. It meant that in the dry heat of the day, loading this "hay" into the hayrack where it would be piled and tamped down tight and later stacked at the hay corral near the barn. We were subject to scratches, abrasions and dusts in the process. Always vigilant for rattlesnakes we stepped lightly on these occasions.

As children we always looked forward to rain clouds because of the benefits that it gave the crop yield but also, it meant that we could go to town for shopping, movies, and to see our friends. The mud roads posed interesting navigational challenges. Muddy roads with their ruts, blue gumbo, and yellow clay brought exciting road trips.

We usually stayed in town until the roads were wetted and "hard" making them safer to travel on. Uncle Rueben, when asked how he drove on muddy roads, stated that he just drove as fast as he could. That way he didn't have time to go into the ditch. Seemed to work for him. Although in today's world maybe we should consider other alternatives.

Winter storms were a challenge also. It most generally meant that we stayed inside a lot of the time. The very small houses we occupied while growing up became very confining to us boys. There was no TV. Only sporadic radio reception was received on our small sets. Very few books, magazines, or newspapers were available. Only a couple of board and card games were our recreation most of the time. When we became too noisy, which happened often, the folks would say it was time to go outside to play or gather the eggs, feed the chickens, water and milk the cow. Noise time was chore time automatically! A suggestion that chore time was near quickly brought a deafening quiet to all activity. That is, until the arguments arose as to whose turn it was to do the chores. This conflict was quickly settled by sending us all out together. Funny thing, exposure to 10-20 below zero temperatures will solve most any problem or argument. Maybe our State Department could use this method in settling global disputes?

The heartache that weather brought to the farming community cannot be described in words. Having risked all time, effort, and money on that wheat crop only to see grasshoppers by the millions devour the green stalks or see a black thunder cloud advance from the northwest bringing high winds and sheets of hail stealing away the crop was a gut wrenching experience. I can still see Dad going out in the field with the hail insurance adjuster seeking what was left. Hoping against all hope that the hail missed the good stand of grain just over the hill. Wrong. The devastation most generally was widespread. We lost it all. These times did create character in us, however, and we relied on our faith that we would survive some way, some how. Giving up or surrendering to adversity was not in our vocabulary or makeup.

Rainbows were a phenomenon that we encountered following God's blessing in the form of rain. We always had heard that there was a pot of gold to be found at the end of the rainbow. Don't believe that. We never found it as described but we found something better, a communion with God and a bonding that lasts to this day. He is always there rain or shine. But especially when it rained.

The Northern Lights, Aurora Borealis, were rarely seen but on those occasions we observed reds and greens from these displays in the ionosphere caused by magnetic and other occurrences of ionized atmospheric gases. So they tell us today. The lights were as mysterious to us as they were to the Native Americans who passed these way centuries before us.

We would spend many hours gazing into the summer and winter sky as children. We would try to imagine seeing animals and pictures made by the rolling clouds in the blue sky. There is nothing quite like prairie skies in providing animated entertainment. Certainly, sheepherders sitting on sand rocks while watching their flocks were also occupied by this never-ending display in the early years.

## RELIGION:

Attending Trinity Lutheran Church in Wibaux was a treat but the service was extremely difficult to sit still through for us children. Upon command the blue hymnals were brought out and the voices of about 35 faithful people were raised led by the out of tune foot pedal operated reed organ located near the pulpit. Whenever possible, we kids would sit in the back pew near the oil burner stove alongside Granddad Trollope. He would chew Copenhagen snuff, spit in a coffee can and smile down on us during the service. "What A Friend We Have In Jesus" still seems to resonate whenever we pass that corner where now stands the new church we built in

1954. "Holy, Holy . . ." was another of Granddads favorites. In the old church during the spring thaw, water accumulated to a depth of about six inches on the walkway to the front entrance. Wooden planks placed over this pond allowed us to walk over the water to the church. It was kind of our version of the Red Sea experience in Bible times, I guess. Hide and seek play in the church was a great treat. Some of us would hide behind the altar. This was about the best place to hide in the old church building, which consisted of the sanctuary, altar, and a side room that served as a very small kitchen. After school, hungry kids would come boiling into the church where the Ladies Aid meetings were held. This meant a wonderful supper would be waiting for us. The ever-present hamburger goulash was especially favored along with fresh rolls, milk and coffee. Oh, don't forget the cake and cookies. The old church, which had been purchased from the Episcopalians in the late 1930's, was torn down and replaced with the current structure in the early 1950's. Original construction of the old church probably dated back to the 1880's. Demolition took place, followed by pouring cement, planting trees, and building a frame church complete with a basement currently used today. Next door a two-story parsonage was constructed and a fine new pastor and his wife were called to serve the congregation of about 100 members.

We all sinned while growing up. We all told "fibs" to save one's skin or to make oneself bigger than life. Seems these prevarications always were found out and exposed. Especially if it involved adults. Kids tended to believe unquestionably everything that was told to them or what was heard on the streets, classroom, movies, or elsewhere. I remember one of the times that I was caught believing what was told to me when one of my classmates had a pencil that didn't have any paint on it. It had been scored and carved up a bit. I asked him where he got a pencil like that and he remarked that it came from a tree branch and that all one had to do is to break off a branch, sharpen it in the pencil sharpener to begin writing your assignments. That was how pencils could be fashioned! It took a long time before I questioned that. But even today, when a tree twig is encountered I think of it as a pencil. Santa Claus and the Easter Bunny were myths perpetuated for years. Monsters and ghost stories abounded. Older children usually told these tales to the younger set. Is this the beginning of discernment and questioning of authority that became a hallmark of Montanans?

Fibs, lies, and distortions could fill the rest of this book. The main point is that before they were exposed some pain, sleepless nights, worry and discomfort were suffered until confession and reconciliation time came around. We found that it was better to fess up to the truth and face the circumstances that to perpetrate deceit and ignorance. Repentant sinners always received forgiveness.

Camping out under the stars was not a common occurrence but there were some experiences that come to mind. At the Lutheran Bible Camp in Absorka Mountains we camped out on cots alongside of the overcrowded log cabins. We woke up to a strange sound one morning convinced that the noise was coming from roaming bears and well they might have been. Deep concern welled up in us. Somehow we no longer felt snug in our cots. Something just short of panic was developing until we found that squirrels and the sound of the river, stream, and the woods waking up to the warmth of the new day caused the commotion. It gets cold sleeping out on a mountainside but the air is clear and crisp.

No question about it, the happiest memory as a youth was being with our friends at the Lutheran Bible Camp at Absorka Mountains. This site was located some miles up a river canyon from Big Timber, Montana. Singing, studying, playing, hiking, camping out, log cabins, animals, woods, ghost town exploration, games made that weeklong experience a cornerstone in my love of the outdoors, people, and gave an excellent background in religion.

During camping trips we would also instigate a snipe hunt. On one occasion at Bible Camp we began talking about the values of snipe hunting. Six of us in the log cabin decided to promote a snipe hunt.

One of the fellows in our cabin was a little homesick and we campers began to pick on him somewhat. As we were lying there in beds and we started to talk about snipe hunting. He didn't know what that was. We told him it was easy just to go out side and look around for snipes. Hearing boots hit the floor and the screen door closing he left us. We didn't hear from him for a while and it got very quiet in the cabin. We all were frightened that he might have gotten lost. It was a dark night in that remote part of the mountains. Finally to everyone's relief he came wandering back. We were not quite certain who bore the brunt of this trick. He reported, of course, that no snipes were found. We were all happy about that! It did cure his homesickness, however. He was now a part of the group.

Our family was religious. We attended Trinity Lutheran Church services; Sunday school every Sunday and our youth group Luther League meetings. Big Sunday dinners and movies were a part of our weekends. I remember one Sunday we went to church after Mom put a pressure cooker filled with chicken and noodles on the stove. We could hardly wait to get back to savor this delicacy. When we opened the kitchen door we found that the pressure cooker had exploded, spraying chicken parts, fat, noodles, and water all over the place. Not only did we have to settle for lesser fare, but also the clean up was laborious.

Special events at Easter were the usual egg hunts and the Easter Bunny would leave candy in little nests that we left for him around the house. The nests were constructed of tea towels rolled up and placed on chairs. Church breakfasts of eggs with all of the trimmings were served after the early morning church services. Croquette was played in the early springtime chill at Scammon's house until the second church service was conducted later on in the morning.

On our bedroom wall hung a blue iridescent cardboard picture with a prayer, "Now I Lay Me Down To Sleep, I Pray The Lord My Soul To Keep, If I Should Die Before I Wake, I Pray The Lord My Soul To Take." We all remember looking at this picture as we drifted off to sleep on the chenille bedspread covered bed at naptime. A version of that prayer plaque is found on my office wall even today.

Probably the biggest influences in our lives included a Lutheran Pastor, Loyal E. Golf (Religion); a science teacher, (Dedication); history teacher, (Humanity); coach (Sportsmanship); farm hand, (Philosophy); Dad, (Work Ethic & Love), Mom, (Love & Independence); Sunday School Teachers (Religion); and 4-H Leaders ("Can Do" attitudes). Of course, grandparents, aunts, uncles, cousins all influenced us in countless ways. It certainly took a village to raise kids in those days.

# WAR:

As a boy of about 4 years old I was sitting on the front step of our rented farmhouse looking into the blue sky seeing contrails from a highflying plane. I ran to Mom asking if the Japanese were coming. We forget that even small children are influenced by war and they begin to develop fears and prejudice at early ages. During wartime we would go to town to partake of the patriotic celebrations and to see soldiers dressed in their uniforms especially on Veteran's Day. War came to Wibaux in other ways. WWII we knew was not pleasant because we did not have any candy or hardly any toys due to rationing and war material shortages. In that war even kids on isolated ranches suffered. At the same time we felt very vulnerable. We had no concept of the world or what the global problem was. Soldiers were guarding the railroad bridge in Wibaux to prevent saboteurs from blowing it up causing disruption of transportation. Military personnel evidently were quartered in railroad cars on the rail siding near the grain elevator buildings. I don't think that there was much danger of the enemy messing around Wibaux, though. Strangers would be identified immediately, I am certain. Another visible sign of WWII was the rationing of meat, sugar, shoes, tires, gasoline, and a whole host of material goods. The Federal Office Price Administration governed rationing. Today, I sit on a different door stoop in another city, looking into the sky. Even at my advanced age, I still cannot fathom why those planes are still flying high leaving contrails as they head for another part of the world at war. Dad couldn't fathom this either and his poem showing this concern is presented in the final pages of this book.

WWII brought all kinds of memories. Going to town to hear war news was important. There was no TV and radio reception was limited. I remember VJ (Victory In Japan) Day most of all. Everyone was happy. There were soldiers in uniform. Flags, parades, cheering and happy times.

Some of the celebrations that took place in Wibaux will be remembered for years. The Memorial Day march though town by the veterans and the high school band. Hearing speeches in the park and volleys of gunfire salutes at the cemetery and on the Beaver Creek Bridge were ritual in memory of the war dead and all those pioneers who had gone before us. Our family would travel to various cemeteries decorating graves with fruit jars containing cut lilac flowers in water. We all would stand over the graves, discuss the deceased person and his or her life. I am certain that if they could have heard and seen us on those ceremonial days, they would have been proud. The fact that they were gone but not forgotten was important to the survivors also.

When the cold war came and national defense was at its height in everyone's minds, elaborate measures were taken to protect the citizens of our area. The old Stair coalmine north of Wibaux was designated as a nuclear shelter in case of Russian bombing attacks. In Beach a watchtower was constructed on a downtown building and Civil Defense volunteers manned it to keep vigil for incoming enemy aircraft. The cold war never became a "hot" war and no aircraft to cause us harm invaded our airspace.

Today, a section of the Wibaux Cemetery is designated to our veterans. As we pass by these stones memories flood us all who are left.

# DOGS AND CATS:

Every farm had a dog and cats. Cats ate mice. No mice. No rattlesnakes was the logic. Farm dogs were important in alerting us of nearby skunks, snakes, and other varmints that might happen along the farmstead. Farm dogs also were the child sitters. Parents could look out the window, see the dog and know that the kids were not far away. Our dog's name was "Tippie." We never did name the cats. I guess that they either were not recognized as being too important or for some reason did not last long on the ranch. Some met up with foxes, coyotes, and skunks and were probably bested in combat. Remember, no dogs or cats in the house! That was true until we received a Cocker Spaniel pup that was allowed to stay inside the mudroom of the house. It was not too long, however, that Ginger was given a name and had the run of the house and she became like one of the family.

Sometimes farm dogs would meet up with a skunk and the odor was just awful. It was a miserable experience for both the dog and the family. Usually, when this happened we would see the dog run under the granary to hide out for a day or two while "airing out". It was a time of ostracism or self-banishment from the "clan." At other times the dog would encounter a porcupine and would come home with a nose full of quills. Talk about painful! We used pliers from the workshop to pull these quills out. Not an easy task for all concerned.

# TURKEYS AND CHICKENS:

Raising turkeys was quite a task. Some years there were about ten of them. We raised these birds and they grew up weighing probably 23-24 pounds. One year a big thunderstorm descended, heavy rain flooded the yard drowning our turkeys as they bunched up around the pump house. Some did not make it to Thanksgiving that year. Turkeys posed problems sometimes. Gobblers would strut and attack you when you least expected it. It was a joy to watch those big birds chase and eat grasshoppers. Their heads would bob and their necks would crane while seeking out their prey. These critters were welcome farm animals most of the time, however it seemed that their personalities mirrored those of the cats on the ranch being fiercely independent and territorial.

Gathering eggs was a chore that fell to us kids. We would venture into the chicken house searching for eggs that the old hens had laid in their open-faced, straw lined orange crate nests. Hens occupying the warm nests required careful probing to obtain the precious eggs under their carcasses. In this probing we opened ourselves up to a peck and flapping wings from the protective chickens as the dust and feathers flew. There is a term commonly used explaining this activity in allegorical terms, "being as protective as a mother hen on the nest," or just categorizing someone as a bitty old hen overly concerned over details. In the semi darkness of the hovel's interior there always was the possibility that a snake may have beat you to the hen's nest to raid it of the warm eggs. Reaching into the nest could bring this hazard also. We can never remembering experiencing snakes and eggs exposure but there were pictures of that sort of thing one time in the Successful Farming magazine. In winter, the eggs could be frozen in the nest. Ice cracked open the eggs exposing the interior white and yoke. In the summer our free ranging chickens would nest most anywhere. Gathering eggs could become quite an adventure in locating these out of the way nesting places. Adele tells of finding a treasure trove of eggs in the haystack near the old red barn. She promptly placed the eggs in her bib overalls pockets and crawled beneath the gate on the way to the house on her way to proudly show Mom her discovery. In so doing, she broke the eggs in her pocket necessitating an explanation and an over all clean up. Chickens would eat grasshoppers, grain, grass and water melon seeds us kids would spit out while eating our favorite summer dessert. Many contend that this type of free ranging poultry is healthier and produces a tastier product than the caged variety.

# FARMLIFE:

When eating our dinner there were always some leftovers. One of our hired hands would always be the last to leave the kitchen table. Mom would invite him to refill his plate and eat up the leftovers because as she said he might as well eat them because she was just going feed it to the chickens anyway. "Clean 'er up Bill" was another of the echoes that probably could be heard in our old, crumbling ranch house today.

Fighting over who was to do the chores was a major area of family conflict. Who was going to milk the cow, gather eggs, round up the milk cows from the pasture, feed & water the livestock, and travel to the root cellar to fetch potatoes all caused disruptions in the peace and quiet of the house.

Dad allowed me to drive at the age of 12 years. I would sit behind the steering wheel coasting along as he threw out fence posts from the back of an old International pick up truck. Next came tractor operation. We had an International Harvester Model M that was used to pull a hayrack during threshing operations and during corn cultivating. This was fun at first but it soon became work. While cultivating cornrows on sandy hillsides it was difficult not to have the tractor not slip and slide down between rows tearing out precious corn stalks. While pulling a hayrack being used to haul bundles of wheat to the threshing machine, I made a mistake once and the tractor rolled back a bit causing the wheel of the tractor to back over a worker's foot. Sandy soil and luck prevented this from being a serious injury.

Mom and Dad were hard workers. Mom would help out with the farm work. She did all of the housework, gathered eggs, milked cows, separated cream, raised chickens and turkeys, helped with the feeding of the bum lambs and skim milk calves. When butchering spring chickens Mom had an unusual way of dispatching them. She would grab a chicken by the legs and step on their head while pulling upward thus separating the chicken's body from its head. This was a very effective method of killing chickens. The bird minus its head would flop around and finally remain still. The birds were then scalded in hot water and feathers were plucked from the carcass. Any remaining pinfeathers were singed off using the kitchen-stove flame. The birds were eviscerated, cleaned and placed in cool water ready to be frozen in cardboard ice cream containers. These were sold to the local townspeople for one dollar each providing much of the money to pay for our groceries. We would also trade eggs for groceries at the store.

My father was a great guy. We all loved him a lot. There are good memories of him. We had many good times working on the ranch, attending church, women's club, 4-H, welding on old cars, hauling water with the pick up truck, building the church and parsonage in Wibaux, harvesting grain, mowing hay, hauling bales, spraying weeds, repairing farm equipment, and fixing fence. Planting and harvesting potatoes are some of the great times we had. Good advice I got from Dad was spoken and unspoken. I learned to work hard. Be honest. Don't quit. "Don't forget where you came from." Tomorrow is another day. Love one another. Get an education. Be proud of who you are. I have said on occasion that he instructed us to "Take anything you can get for free and wave at Cadillacs". He probably did not state this last phrase but it does make a good story.

We always had what we needed. Santa Claus was good to us even though we were poor. Air rifles, some toys, .22 caliber rifles, bow and arrows were all special to us when we were growing up. Dad and Mom would take us to the movies, which we enjoyed tremendously. We were all happy with whatever we got.

Our town had two barbers who dictated hairstyles of our youth. Dad would alternate sending us to each of the main street shops for our usual short-cropped coiffure. In high school we had flat top haircuts. The hair was cut very short on the top of our heads and the

sides were left to grow up and were combed back into a "duck butt."
My hair was not like this, however. I had heinies (German short
haircuts) in the summer and short hair that could be combed in the
winter during school sessions. When the weather turned warm we
would be asked, "Are you getting your summer haircut?"

To probably repeat our summer activities while growing up on
the ranch, we spent a lot of time reading comic books, drinking
Kool-Aid, climbing trees, hunting birds and rabbits with a BB gun.
Swimming in ponds, going to town to see friends, attending movies
and picnics. To be redundant, the school bus to Bible Camp from
Glendive to the rural mountainous area where we were greeted with
log cabins, mountains, steams, ghost towns, pine trees, mountain
climbing and good friends. What a wonderful experience this was.
Sleeping outside under the stars on army cots when the cabins were
all full to capacity was a cool but exciting experience.

Our fishing attempts along Beaver Creek did not always pan out
(literally and figuratively). Our improvised fishing tackle was
fashioned from red yarn attached to safety pins as hooks. We did
manage to catch a couple of bullheads with this primitive gear,
however. We cooked the fish on sticks over a campfire. On to better
and more exciting things like smoking Indian tobacco found along
the banks of Beaver Creek. This was terrible stuff. One puff was all
anyone could or would take.

Candy was not readily available in the 1940's until after the War.
There was candy at Christmas time and at Easter time, however.
Christmas candy came from Santa Claus when he made his trip to
Wibaux to greet the children and distribute bags of nuts, fruit and
hard candy to everyone eagerly waiting in line. Chocolate covered
vanilla cream goodies were always there. At Easter, the Bunny would
drop off candies into our nests fashioned from towels. What a joy
to find candy eggs, chocolate bunnies, hard-boiled colored eggs on
Easter morning. Candy availability improved in the early 1950's.
Hershey bars with almonds, Snickers bars, Butterfinger bars, Fire

Stick Candy, licorice, gumballs with colorful packaging was found at the drug and grocery stores. Candy bars cost a nickel with some costing a dime. Gumballs cost a penny. Candy was at a premium during the WWII war years due to the rationing of sugar for the war effort. While candy was a rarity the ever-present popcorn filled the fun food gap. A large wash pan full of yellow popcorn with about a quarter pound of melted homemade butter poured over it with a dash of salt provided an excellent snack while playing Scrabble or Chinese Checkers on a cold winter's afternoon.

In the summer we had a lot of fine picnics. Church, 4-H Club, School, Family Get Togethers, and the Cottonwood Ladies Club were sponsors. We would go along the Beaver Creek, member's homes, at school or church for these affairs. I can just remember vaguely "Old Settlers" picnics that were held. I am not quite certain how one became an old settler. I expect it was a group of early homesteaders who came to this country in the era of about 1906-1918.

Games we played as children and youths included Scrabble, charades, musical chairs, fruit basket upset, button-button whose got the button, Captain May I, ring around the rosy, Simon says, monopoly and checkers. These are parlor games not played much any more.

Heat waves and droughts were commonplace during the 1940's-50's. No electricity was available until REA electrified farms in 1949. Absence of electricity meant no ice, refrigeration or fans for cooling. On one occasion the weather was so hot that we all went to grandma's house to lie on the living room floor with wet washcloths on our foreheads. At this time she had a fan, which moved air about. On other occasions we would fill an old galvanized metal washtub with water climb in and sit in the shade. We would sometimes sit in this tub for hours. Later on the availability of electricity brought choices. We bought a small refrigerator, which was powered by a 100# LPG cylinder to fuel the cooling mechanism and electricity for lighting the interior of the cabinet. While evenings were delightfully cool we could always look forward to the hot sun the next morning.

Humidity was low so even in the middle of the day it was somewhat bearable in the shade out of the sun. Temperatures of about 100 degrees in the daytime cooled to the 70's at night. In front of our house was a root cellar that was filled with ice blocks that had been cut in the winter from the dammed coulee nearby. To keep the ice from melting it was packed tightly with hay, sawdust and straw in the cellar providing cooling for cream, milk, melons and was used to make ice cream on special occasions.

Electrical power outages did not present much of a problem because we didn't have access to electrical power until 1949. It was then that the REC (Rural Electrical Co-Op) came through and wired the farm. Power was dependable but would go off line occasionally following storms. Electricity improved our lives immensely by bringing us power for lights, electric motors, entertainment and modern shop tools for use on the farm.

Farm work was always filled with a certain amount of danger from accidents. I remember shutting my finger in a pick up truck door. Hitting one's finger while pounding nails was a minor incident that occurred on a regular basis. Cuts, sprains, strains, bruises, sunburns, and even a few broken bones were recorded. Falls from horses and high places were a fact of life. Slips and falls, bicycle accidents, and sports injuries were some of the situations that slowed us up a bit. We learned by accident.

Some animals were feared while on the farm. But we were probably scared more times than not by being chased by imaginary animals at night. Snakes, bobcats, etc. There were cantankerous turkeys that would chase us. Sometimes an old horned buck sheep would charge us. Sometimes cows would take after us to protect their calves. Birds would attack us if we neared their nests.

Reading books was a somewhat limited activity during the formative years in elementary school due to the limited availability of reading material. Access to good material was scarce due to the lack of current books and magazines in the city and school libraries. Tom Sawyer & Hardy Boys mysteries were favorites. Of course there were the comic books that we received from our cousins. I remember one time when we were given a rather large box of comic books we had a heyday reading those stories. If we had those comic books today, they would be priceless. We all would be rich.

## FAMILY:

Ethnicity of our family includes: Trollope—England. Stockwell-England. Amunrud-Norway. There are family tree documents available that would give more information. The Stockwell branch came to this country in the 1600's. The Davis family-England also in the early 1600's. The Trollope's arrival has been difficult to pinpoint but it may be around 1860. The Amunrud's came to Iowa in the mid to late 1800's. Good information concerning family genealogy is found in the Eggebraaten/Elvestuen book, which outlines the Norwegian side. Other bits and pieces of the Trollope, Stockwell, and Davis families are also available.

Today, August 1, 2005, my brother, Stanley Duane died of a heart attack or stroke at his home in Billings, Montana. Needless to say, we are all grieving at his passing. One of the unfinished works we shared was the further compilation of stories from the ranch just as Dad did in his incomplete book. This unfinished work prompts those of us left to be more diligent in the work of chronicling those times so they will not be forgotten for all time. No question about it Dude and Dad's untimely deaths struck us all very hard.

I first saw the light of day in April 1940 at the Golden Valley Hospital in Beach, ND. It is said that the second floor room on the NW corner of this two-story frame building was where mom and I were first quartered. The old hospital building was demolished after 1995 or so. My doctor was Dr. Parrott and his fee for medical services was eight dollars. Mom still has the cancelled check. Hmmm, Dr. Parrott, do you suppose I inherited the gift of gab from this doctor?

Dad drove Mom to the hospital speeding along in a 1928 Chevrolet Coupe during a spring snowfall. In the years that followed our family grew. Alvin Bruce Trollope was born in August, 1941 Stanley Duane Trollope was born in July 1942; Adele Doris was born in December 1950. My brothers and sister are Montanans having been delivered in the Glendive NPBA Hospital. Over the years the ranks of this family have thinned a bit. Alvin Bruce Trollope drowned along with his friend Sandy at a school picnic held at the Wilson Ranch located North of Wibaux on May 20, 1954. As I write this, Stanley Duane Trollope died at the age of 63 years of a heart attack on August 1, 2005. His death was just one day before what would have been Alvin's 64th birthday. In life they had shared the same age in years for the period of July 23 until August 2.

Doris Mabel, Mom, was born in a farmhouse near Beach, ND in December 1920. Stanley Arden, Dad, was born in a farmhouse north of Wibaux, Montana in June 1918. They were married in June, 1939.

My first name was given as Loraine. But everyone called me "Rainy". Some would call me "Rain In The Face". For the first thirty or so years I misspelled my first name. Lorraine was spelled with two "r's" making it a girl's name. Grandma Alberta would always spell it correctly and she contended that I was in error using the double "r". She was right so finally my name was revised to read the same as my birth certificate. I had an attorney in the 1970's contact schools, college, Social Security, etc. to correct the spelling.

Nicknames in our family included: Duane-"Dude", Adele-" Griddly (Because of a teddy bear called Grizzly), Alvin was called "Alkali" and Stanley Arden, Dad, "Rab". Ma was called Ma.

In 1950, Adele joined us boys in our family adventures. I was sitting in the gymnasium during a class when my fifth grade teacher came in to announce that I had a sister. Couldn't believe it because I didn't have one when we left for school that cold December morning. Surprise! Adele took a liking to horses and had a Shetland pony and a large old horse that was as gentle as a lamb. Her pet Cocker Spaniel, Ginger followed her everywhere. She picked up quickly doing chores and added her influence to our gang. No doubt about it, she became about the most doted over kid in the county. I expect that is because she earned it.

Dad had a real challenge in providing for us all. He was a farmer/rancher, construction worker, heavy equipment operator, country extension agent, deputy sheriff, probation officer, corn salesman, custodian in a school and hospital, Justice of the Peace-Judge just to list a few of the occupations that were required to keep us on the farm. In some years hail, grasshoppers, drought, heat, plant disease, and other calamities would take our lush crops leaving us with few sources of income. Cattle prices usually would bail us out and the banker would agree to finance us for another year.

One of the major influences in our lives as we grew up was the importance of movies. We would attend at least two or three movies per week at the Bijou Theatre in Beach or at the Wibaux Theatre. From movies we learned history, manners, speech, social graces, government, psychology and teamwork. We still are fans of the cinema no matter what the subject matter. Pathe news showed snippets of the war effort along with whatever news was judged to be important. In those days editorial comment or talk show jargon was not heard. There was basically a single voice and a single viewpoint extolled. This ended up with subsequent excesses involving McCarthyism and other incendiary movements in our Nation's history.

Mom was kept busy raising us kids, running the household and contributing to the farm work that had to be done. She did get a job at the local Drug Store when her domestic duties load lightened. Her work did not bring in great sums of money but she soon learned to delight in her retail work at the store. She held this job for many years. I have seen her account book which lists of hours worked and wages received. In later years Mom took a position as a cook at the Nursing Home. She spent over 25 years in this avocation rising to the position of Director of Food Service. She loved cooking for others taking great care to provide quality food for the residents. Many seminars and training sessions were attended so that she became a real professional in the dietary profession.

Our family did not move around. We lived in Wibaux on a rented farmstead known as the Tom Parker place located east of town north of old U.S. Hwy 10 bridge along Beaver Creek near where the Welcome Center is located today. This included a single bedroom house, barn, garage, chicken house, root cellar, an outhouse and about 4 acres of land. Rent was $20.00 per month. We lived in this house during school sessions, moving back to the farm in the summer. It was extremely unusual for us to travel more than 50 miles from home in those years. One trip to Yellowstone Park was about the only major trip we took until we began attending Bible Camp in the mountains near Big Timber, Montana in our teenage years. When asked why the family did not travel in those years, Mom replied that we just did not have the money. We lived in two other locations in Wibaux. The small house located across the street from the New High school and the McClain/Elliott houses near the Lutheran Church where Mom still lives. Our farmhouse is deteriorated to an unlivable condition.

Vacation trips were few and far between. We went to Yellowstone Park at least once, however. We stayed at my uncle's house in Bozeman and in several log cabin motels along the way. While in the Park we stopped to observe some black bears. One of the bears rose up on his hind legs and leaned against the car window near where I was sitting. Kind of scary. He left claw marks on the door's paint. We saw the usual Yellowstone landmarks, Yellowstone Inn, Old Faithful, mud pots, animals, and the mountains. It was one of the finest outings our family ever had. To show how "pure" the water was, Dad drank from a small roadside stream. Not certain if that should be repeated in today's environment. Even the waters of the pristine National Parks are in question due to the possible contamination from animals, people, and industry.

Aunt Norma hosted me along with their family, which included their three children and myself during a part of the school year. This is how I spent much of the first grade of elementary school. We lived in a rented room in the Bushman home, which was located across the street from the current Amsler Convenience Store. It was very crowded. I occupied an army cot set up in a small closet next to the electric hot plate, which was setting on a wooden orange crate. This constituted the sum total of the kitchen cooking facilities. There was no kitchen sink or refrigerator. It was here that I first saw cold cereal served in its individual cardboard box. Cut along the dotted lines, fold back the cardboard and carefully clip the waxed paper before adding cold milk and a little sugar. Then the feast began! Lunch was food cooked on the hot plate. I believe soup may have been the usual fare. Sleeping in this rented room near old Hwy 10 sometimes was difficult because of the road noise. Trucks would pass by in seemingly large numbers to this young country lad

Memories of Granddad John included farming operations, shearing sheep, branding cattle, threshing using horse drawn wagons and old threshing machines. Stories about gathering and breaking wild horses and the hardships they went through on the prairie would almost bring tears to our eyes. When we stayed overnight at Grandma's house, she would place a large feather tick on the floor near the stove and we boys would burrow into the warm feathers, which protected us against the cool draft of the farmhouse. Grandma had an asparagus fern in an old dented cooking pot hanging from the ceiling over the kitchen table. It was her pride and joy. But it was always an aggravation to Dad who once took out his jack knife and cut off a rather large branch when Grandma Trollope wasn't looking. Seems as though that brought a retort from Alberta. Unfortunately it probably was the only green thing growing around the ranch in some of those dry years.

Granddad Dan and Grandma Mabel were a lot of fun for us. We had a lot of cousins and we would all get together at their house at holiday times. Playing Chinese checkers, Scrabble, Old Maid card games, eating popcorn and spending cold winter days in the warmth of their old farmhouse are memories that will last forever. The grandchildren were continually raiding grandma's candy dish, which was kept in the front room china closet. Home cooking, games and sleeping upstairs in the old four-poster metal bed were all special treats. Granddad would dance jig and sing "High Diddle The Cat And The Fiddle . . ." for us. He had a curious habit of pouring his coffee from his cup into a saucer, blowing on the hot black liquid before sipping it loudly.

Since the family was so interdependent for survival, this group could almost be termed a clan. Favorite aunts included Jeanette who used to bring us candy and toys whenever she would visit coming from her work and home in Glendive. Aunt Maye used to play games and sing with us. Her specialty was baking doughnuts and a wonderful sponge cake all of which we devoured at a single sitting.

Aunt Polly would invite us to their family Christmas parties and to church in Beach, ND. These were happy times. They provide many memories of Christmas. The food, fun and games that went along with being with the North Dakota cousins were wonderful times.

Favorite meals included fried chicken, cherry pie, mashed potatoes, gravy, bread and vegetables. For breakfast fried eggs, bacon, pancakes, orange juice, toast, and a big bowl of Wheaties. Deer, antelope, venison, pheasants and side pork were all served on an occasional basis. Beef and pork roasts were a real treat. Chicken and homemade dumplings were second only to Mom's fried chicken. Most generally, food choices were limited. We always had enough to eat. Food was important in our family life. We all gathered around the table to eat fried potatoes, canned or fresh vegetables, eggs, milk, side pork, store bought bread, real butter, ice cream, cake, cookies and pie. Sometimes we would have bread and gravy along with side pork as the main course. I remember one winter that someone had left the root cellar door open and the pile of potatoes in the cool, dark interior had frozen. This was a near disaster because they had been counted on for being the basis for much of our food for the winter. We cooked the frozen potatoes, found that they developed a pink color and tasted sweet. This is probably due to the frost evidently transforming the starch in the potato to sugar. Ear corn was picked from our farm cornfields. It had a heavy starchy taste. Great food, though. In season, deer and antelope venison provided a departure from chicken and side pork meats served. Wild plums, buffalo berries, and chokecherries gathered from the pasture were used to make jams and jellies.

Movies and radio programs provided much of our entertainment. Radio programs included The Shadow, Gang Busters, The Green Hornet, The FBI, Amos & Andy, Fibber McGee & Mollie and others were the highlight of our evenings and Sunday afternoons. Movies that I remember most are "Sgt. York", "So Dear To My Heart", and "The Ten Commandments."

Back home in Montana during the 1950's life was a simpler. One weekly newspaper, one radio station in Glendive, a library filled with outdated books, traveling salesmen, county extension agent, and the preacher were our sources of values and information. A few paved roads, daily trains, RFD Postal Service and a Greyhound bus were our connections with the outside world. The biggest political race was who was running for Sheriff. Although, the school board elections were also important. In our community, the main news consisted of who was born, who got married, and who died. Nobody knew what the weather would be. It was endured as a part of being a Montanan. During war times, the question was, "Who's Going?" Seems as though, when they went they didn't come back. If they survived the battles, they stayed in California or Washington. Some went off to college and were lured by large salaries and the bright lights of the city. These are the same attitudes and values that continue today in areas of the Southwest, Midwest, South, and West. Most Montanans will deny that change is happening. They will not accept or consider how change will impact them. Politically, they will vote for the candidate who presents the lesser threat and not for the candidate who may provide the greater promise. Politicians who fail to learn this fact will continue to be in the losing column. Change is to be avoided even if change appears to be the most reasonable course of action. Ooops, must stop here or this document will become perforated with political policies that perpetrate today's preferences.

As kids, we learned at an early date that we had to stand up for ourselves. There was no use to run to Mom for help unless it was of a serious nature. Oh, there were times in which the older cousins would tend to pick on us and engage in a bit of fun but we learned that they meant well and their shenanigans were tolerated.

Special celebrations at school included Valentines Day. Classmates exchanged Valentine cards and we were served cup cakes and chocolate cake along with Kool Aid at school parties. Some of the Valentines had lollipop candies attached. We would keep score to see who got the most candies. Valentines made out of red construction paper having a paper doily glued on its face. Crayon addresses with best wishes personalized the card.

Our favorite time of the year was summer. We enjoyed the sun and fun plus independence and freedom. Winter was great, too. Playing in snow, ice-skating, shooting and hunting rabbits, digging snow caves and exploring the great outdoors kept us busy. Being outside sure beat being cooped up in the small house we had at the time.

On my tenth birthday party, a number of my friends came over to the house. And as is usual at any children's parties there were antics taking place almost continually. While eating sandwiches, Dale held up a sandwich, which I shot out of his hand with my rubber tipped dart gun. The sandwich flew apart resulting in a loud cheer from everyone.

Chores we had included outdoor and indoor varieties. Vacuuming and cleaning floors. Cleaning the kitchen sink. Picking up papers, hanging up clothes and sometimes washing dishes were household chores that fell to us kids. Outdoor farm chores included fixing fence, feeding and watering livestock, cleaning the barn and chicken house, hauling hay & grain, operating the combine, harvesting, shoveling grain, cutting hay, branding calves, milking cows, gathering eggs, rounding up livestock, cleaning the shop and painting the barn were activities that we enjoyed most. There was always work to do. We didn't look at it as work, though. It was just stuff that had to be done.

Mother's Day was a big celebration. We would make mom special cards as a school project. We would hide them until Mother's Day and then give them to her on that Day. Sometimes we'd go out to dinner. Sometimes mom would cook a regular meal at home. Favorite TV shows were Gilligan's Island, old 1930's movies; barn dance shows, local programming including polka bands, Superman, serials, Roy Rogers & western movies.

One of the first family reunions was a four-generation picnic at the Air Drome Picnic grounds north of Wibaux in about 1944. We had a picture taken of Great Granddad J.E. Trollope, Granddad John C. Trollope, and Dad Stanley Arden Trollope and myself. The photo is found among our treasures. Four generations were a novelty in those days.

In a way, family reunions occurred every holiday. Lots of food, kids playing and conducting mischief was the order of the day. Good times always were had by all. One of the biggest of all our family reunions was held at the Christian Fundamentalist Church (CF Church) in March of 1955. That occasion was the 50th wedding anniversary of Dan & Mabel Stockwell, all of the cousins, aunts, uncles, and relatives of every stripe attended. A religious service was held with several of the grandchildren participating in various musical renditions. One of the lingering memories of that affair was the perception of the old age of Grandma and Granddad. Now, as I approach their age at that time, they seem to be quite young.

There has been a lot of talk about family values lately. Nobody, I have met, can give me a good definition. I guess we got our values from observing my folks and grandparents. These portrayed nonverbal rules. No utterance of any voice is as loud as "do as I do". In those days families spent much time together and the houses were smaller. Maybe one TV or one radio provided the entertainment choices. There were limited options. Everyone had a hand in completing the chores that were required. There was a sharing and discussion of conditions found while completing the chores. There is now a multiplicity of activities each family member takes part in outside of the home. These activities separate family members. We are not closely involved in each other's experiences resulting in decreased opportunities to interact with family members. Much of the "glue" holding the family together is lost. They say that families that pray together stay together. A new slogan appears to be required: "families that spend time together, stay together and children learn the rules of both the home and society.

## WORK:

My first real job was at the age of about 14 years. I worked at the neighbor's farm while they were on vacation. The job involved feeding chickens, milking cows and separating cream from the milk. When they returned a few days later. I stayed on to help their hired carpenter, old Tom, install sheetrock on the farmhouse ceiling. Pay was about five dollars per day. I expect that that was about four dollars too much for all the help I provided. Although the "employer" was pleased with the work that was done as Tom was very crippled up with arthritis and any assistance was greatly appreciated. My job was to help hold up the sheetrock ceiling sections while he nailed them in place. Tom was also stone deaf even though he wore a very large battery operated hearing aid. He slept in his station wagon and one morning when he came in for breakfast he had a smile on his radiant face like nobody had seen before. When asked why he was so happy, he said that he had heard thunder during the storm that night.

Tom was quite a hunter and he demonstrated his powerful deer rifle one evening. He raised the gun, sighted in on a cedar fence post some thirty yards distant and let fly with the lead. The bullet hit the post squarely almost severed it in two. I expect that later the next job was to fix the fence.

When I was younger there were no jobs to be had. But luckily there was plenty of work to do around the farm. Field work, chores, feed cattle, gather eggs, clean barns and chicken houses, milk cows, brand cattle, work in the fields at harvest time, haul hay bales. But there were no McDonald's or fast food places hiring young people. The only job was sacking groceries at the three stores in town. There were only two positions open and they were spoken for long before we hit town.

We learned at an early age the difference between looking for a job and looking for work. Some people look for a job that doesn't involve work while others look for a job and consider the activity required almost as a recreational pursuit.

When we reached the age of 18-19-20 there was some work available in the construction of a Lincoln Elementary school building in Beach and building the bridge over Interstate I-94 on the west end of Wibaux. This amounted to shoveling wet concrete, tying steel, assembling cabinets, truck driving, site cleanup and general labor. Then came our big job in the oil fields. The project was to lay twelve miles of salt-water transite (asbestos) pipe in a six feet deep trench. The pipe was 4" and 6" in diameter and came in about ten foot lengths. Work involved digging with shovels, running a jackhammer, following the Barber-Greene ditching machine, directing traffic and installing pipe underground. This was dangerous as there were snakes and sometimes a stray deer in the ditch. Ditch collapses were common. No injuries occurred as a result, happily. Oil field angels must have been on the site. Disputes among the workers were another hazard that had not contemplated when we first signed up. Most of us were so tired from working and overheated to move out of the shade at lunch to intervene in any disagreements between workers.

I was fortunate to have been hired by the USDA Agricultural Stabilization & Conservation Dept. in Wibaux County during the summers in my college years. Work included measuring wheat fields, inspecting grass seeding, conservation practices and grain storage bins. This required calling on the county's farmers, completing forms, measuring fields and writing reports. No question about it, this allowed me to attend college and to develop a skill that was valuable throughout my later career in sales and insurance field underwriting/safety. Making calls, discussing business operations, reporting, promoting sales, and conducting public relations campaigns were to be a major part of my insurance and safety occupation for years. Prevention of injury and loss became my life's work being employed by insurance companies and the National Safety Council. Needless injury and fatal incidents became almost an obsession with me in my work organizing safety councils, writing, and promoting safety through insurance inspections, safety training sessions, and presentations.

## SCHOOL:

School brought a plethora of mischievous adventures. One stunt we engaged in was to go out during recess, locate wild onions growing in the field, eat as many as possible, stuffing the rest in our pockets. The school bell would ring calling us back to the third grade classroom as we marched back to work and study. Classrooms were very warm and ventilation was nil. Each of us boys would pant our onion-laced breath and unload his onions into the desks. It was not long before the air was permeated with onion smells much to the displeasure of the teacher and to the delight of the students.

During recess we would play marbles, mumblypeg, slide on the playground slide, swing on the heavy-duty swing set, play baseball, and ride bicycles. Jousting was a vigorous sport we engaged in. This involved one boy sitting on the shoulders of an other while jousting with others for the purpose of knocking them down to the ground. This was popular until my brother, Dude, suffered a compound fracture to his arm in a fall during this play. He was treated in the NPBA Hospital in Glendive at a cost to our parents of eighty dollars. "Dude" sported a cast on his arm for several weeks. This minor accident did not slow up the rest of us, though.

Playing marbles meant tossing our "steelie" shooter into a series of holes in the ground. The pot was in the center and around this pot were located holes in the four corners and directly above and beneath and on both sides of the "pot". By anteing up one marble into the pot and tossing your "steelie" toward the pot, you would collect all the marbles in the pot if you were lucky. I believe in the corner holes the player had to ante up one more marble to the pot. Those who were lucky enough to get their steelie to fall in the other holes took out one marble from the pot. Sound easy. It was for the older players who ended up taking marbles from the younger players. Too bad, you lose. Our first lesson in gambling. First time we lost our marbles.

Mumblypeg was played with your pocketknife. If your knife failed to stick in the ground when tossed, you had to cut yourself. We played this game only infrequently.

One lesson concerning electricity we engaged in and miraculously resulted in no injury. Out behind the school was a basement stairwell having an open electrical socket. We all would line up holding hands while one of the fellows stuck his finger in the socket. It was rumored that only the last person on this line would feel the shock from this activity. I cannot remember if anybody felt that "tingle." We learned that being the last in line was not beneficial in other venues also.

School went on rain, cold, snow or shine. I cannot remember anytime when we were lucky enough to escape the classroom due to weather. I am certain that there were times when they did shut down, however. Oh, there were the times when someone would flush apples and other things down into the toilets causing sewer back ups or there were times when there was no water at the school due to a possible water main break. These events brought a reprieve from the usual mundane schoolwork.

My favorite subject in school was chemistry. While in high school we conducted some rocketry experiments launching rockets into the air. One of my friends went on to be a rocket scientist type as a result of this activity. We ordered out powdered sulfur and powdered zinc, which we packed into steel pipes having nose cones and fins. These "rockets" were set on a wooden board, having an exposed nail that was wired to a battery, coil and switch. When the switch was closed a sparking arc would be produced and ignition of the fuel took place. The rocket would fly several hundred into the air. One time we set this launching up in an abandoned schoolhouse near our farm with many fellow students and towns people in attendance. One rocket, the smaller of the two, made a rapid climb leaving a smoke trail. The other rocket, which was about two feet long, rose to approximately 20 feet and fell on its side, and slid along the grassy prairie finally ending up tangled in a barbed wire fencing material. This was Wibaux County High School's answer to the Russian Sputnik satellite program that ignited the United State's efforts to place a man on the moon. The Federal government encouraged math and science in the study when they instituted the NDSL (National Student Defense Loans) program to produce the needed scientists for the space race. These governmental loans were instrumental in funding education for myself and other fellow students.

Writing has always been an activity that I was involved in. Our 4-H club work required progress reports for our record books. In the seventh grade I wrote a ""Voice Of Democracy" essay for the VFW Auxiliary. This represented my first real success in writing. I won the class prize of $3.00 and received some recognition for this work. I still have a copy of it somewhere. I believe that it was published in the Wibaux Pioneer Gazette circa 1953.

There were a number of really dedicated teachers whom we all respected. They were so instrumental in not only teaching their assigned subjects but helping us along our way while we were growing up. Whatever thanks they received probably did not measure up to their worth to us all.

Our school days gave multiple opportunities for drama, acting, and entertainment venues. Junior High School plays, Senior High School plays, 4-H programs, musical programs of all types for Christmas required participation by almost everyone. Church Christmas programs provided speaking parts and singing. I played Santa in the first program that I can remember. I must have been about 10 years old at the time. Skinny as I was, I wonder who was in charge of casting. One other time early on, I did a tap dance to the tune "Bicycle Built For Two." It was not long after that; I realized that ballet dancing was not my gift. Another time I played a part in a mystery play and don't forget the minstrel show we put on in black face make up at school. This type of minstrel show would be unconscionable today but at age of about 11 years in the early1950's, we just thought it was a normal thing. That was probably due to the fact that we did not have any discrimination toward anybody. That had to be learned elsewhere at a later time.

While recess and lunchtime was our favorite subjects at school we would sometimes have trouble getting back to class on time. Sometimes we would stray over to the creek to throw rocks, catch fish, swim etc. Needless to say there were some mad dashes getting back to the schoolhouse on time. There were two bells that were rung at the close of the lunch hour. The first bell rang fifteen minutes to one o'clock and the final bell was rung promptly at one o'clock. To run the quarter mile in fifteen minutes put us in shape for football, baseball, and basketball in later years.

While in school I played a little basketball and football. I never was chosen for the first team, however. There were too many fantastic athletes in my class. They could run faster, jump higher and understand sports fundamentals better than I could. School sports always were fun, though. If not on the bench waiting to get into the game, you probably would find me in the pep band blaring away on a clarinet. There were times, however, at the barbershop and at other times when people would discuss the athletic prowess of Longhorn high school players in their individual accomplishments while those of us sitting on the bench were not mentioned. This was the first real sting of discrimination felt for many of us third stringers.

My newspaper writing began when I was Secretary of the Peaceful Valley 4-H Club. I published the minutes of our meetings in the Wibaux Pioneer Gazette. It was a joy to see our thoughts in print in that weekly paper. The skills learned there served me well throughout the succeeding years as an insurance investigator-safety engineer and later as a blogger and frequent correspondent to the Letters To The Editor column of the Des Moines Register.

Playground equipment at the school included a swing set, teeter totter, and a slide. The teeter-totter was broken and the boards were deteriorated allowing for sliver injuries. The slide was an old one that was about 15 feet high above the hard surfaced gravel playground. We would sit on wax paper salvaged from our sandwich lunches and this allowed for a very rapid trip down the chute. The swing set was not one of my favorites as I had probably my first epileptic seizure as a first grader while sitting on it while dragging my feet in the accumulated water directly beneath the swing seat. At any rate, when aroused to consciousness I found myself on a bed at my aunt's rented room where we were staying during the school year. I never had an explanation of what happened. About nine years later, however, a repeat performance of a blackout brought medical concerns, which were finally addressed. More about that later.

Music class was about the least impressive class for me. I just never could figure it out. Music required the same skills as mathematics for me. Just did not have an "ear" for music or an "eye" for geometry/ trigonometry. Instrumental music was agreeable to me. I played in the high school band sixth grade through my sophomore year in high school. Clarinet, bass drum, baritone saxophone were the instruments I played.

When in the fifth grade the band teacher asked if I wanted to play in the high school band. She asked what instrument I wanted to play. I said that I would like to play the harmonica. She said that there were no harmonicas in her band. Would I settle for a clarinet? Not knowing what a clarinet was made no difference in my decision to play it. The folks ordered out an old metal clarinet, which they paid $80-90 on a lay away plan from the Dickinson Music House, I believe. I never was very proficient in instrumental music but I always took part and had a great time in the band.

Probably my closest friend during my childhood years was, Rickey. We were in Sunday School, elementary school, and high school and throughout college together. He also played the clarinet. His music acumen was somewhat better that mine, however. We both were third row. I was third chair and I believe he attained the second chair position. We ushered at church every Sunday. There were Luther League meetings, Bible camp and other events that we took part in. He was my debate team partner in college. Chosen to participate in a regional debate tournament in Chicago, we were successful in winning two debates against top notch Wheaton College and one other large school.

Snowball fights could get a little out of hand on occasion. We would choose up sides and the contests became a bit fierce. Usually, little kids got the worst of it because they couldn't throw as far and the size of their missiles were smaller that the "big kids". Some cars were "accidentally" hit during these riotous events.

Sledding and skating became a great venue for letting off steam. The city did not salt, sand or remove snow and ice from the streets in the winter. A solid ice cover made for great ice-skating and sledding on city streets all over town in some years.

Upon graduation from high school, I attended Concordia College in Moorhead, Minnesota. There was cultural shock in this move which included moving to a city that had stop lights, paved roads, running water, warm buildings in the winter, large crowds of people, and a myriad of the other college exposures. College classmates from big towns seemed to have descended from other planets in those days. They had no concept of ranches, horses, or even hard work. Survival of us Westerners meant that we had to group together to promote our own culture. We did this by organizing the Montana Club on campus. Square dancing, music and a pit-roasted beef during a Montana Day celebration gave us all an identity and solidarity.

Again town kids were more advanced than country kids. At college we started out as country kids. We did not stay that way for long though. We studied harder and were more determined than most of the other students.

High school graduation was a very important landmark for me. It meant that there were three choices left for me. They were Army, Farming, or College. Being an epileptic, that automatically narrowed my choices down to one—college. When high school graduation exercises were over, my Dad met with me man to man. He asked what I was going to do, farming or college. I told him that I would be going to college. He agreed that college would be the best course of action but he couldn't help out with the expenses, as there was no money available. Then he said, "There is your bed. It is your bed. You can come back as often as you want and stay as long as you want." I looked over at the old iron spring bed and at the library table, which held an old Royal typewriter in the bedroom knowing full well that I had my work cut out for me. But I also knew that I had the full backing of the family and that if I failed, there was always a place for me.

Our high school was composed of 80-90 students. The class of '58 had nine members. Not many of the graduates went to college in those days but our class was one of the first classes to lead the way to higher education as a large percentage of our senior class of went on to school. High school graduation ceremonies took place in the gym. Commencement speakers all gave glowing remarks about our opportunities suggesting that the world lay at our feet. With our class of nine wearing caps and gowns and the high school band playing "Pomp & Circumstance" we stepped out into an uncertain world. Had we all known what was ahead, we probably would have not stepped so lively. Such was life in May 1958 at age 18.

When we would get together at Luther League, 4-H, and at some family get togethers we would have a joyous time cooking outdoors. We would take aluminum foil, placing sliced onions, carrots, and hamburger paddies inside. These packets then would be placed in the coals and fire where they remained until a fantastic aroma gave indication that the cooking was completed. The packets were retrieved and a veritable feast was enjoyed. Outdoor cooking at other times involved roasting hot dogs and marshmallows following a hay ride or during ice-skating on the creek or farm pond.

Growing up in Montana was a joy. There were some limitations, however. Just exactly what did you wish to be and do when you grew up? Some considerations were: preacher, archeologist, scientist, and just about anything but being a farmer or rancher. My ultimate job occupation ended up being a combination of all of these choices.

School was never my cup of tea. I never could seem to follow what the books were trying to tell me. This was especially true in music and math. The books provided some value to me by prompting and nurturing my own independent thinking. I guess, as a result, they did not teach me what to think but how to think. We did not have free access to books, TV, radio, magazines and newspapers for the main part. Contrast that with today. We have books, newspapers, Internet, videos, cable TV and literature galore. As a result, I take great interest in current events having occasionally been labeled a "news junkie."

At a quite early age, I found that my main interest was in people. That being the case sales, communication, and group participation were very important to me.

Our educational system in those days did not provide counselors or special guidance explaining career opportunities. Few, if any, educational development path considerations were presented to the student. Mentoring was lacking throughout our time in the local schools in those days. This lack of guidance led to a quandary that in several cases was never answered in the graduate's life. At any rate the question: "Where do we go from here?" was never answered. Not to preach on this subject, but if local opportunities could have been presented, it is possible that more youngsters would have stayed and continued calling Wibaux their home. This is just a thought.

## POLITICS:

Politics were not usually a big topic of discussion. Local politics concerning who was running for sheriff, school board, and some of the courthouse offices would be discussed occasionally. I remember that every election evening, townspeople would gather at the Stockman Bar to keep tabs on the large blackboard upon which election results were posted as various voting precincts reported in.

Granddad Dan Stockwell ran for sheriff 1939, just before buying the Peterson place and moving North of Wibaux. Leroy remembers traveling all over the south end of the country with Dan, Earl Baker, who was running for State Senate, and Reuben Amunrud. Rueben knew everyone in the county having worked in the AAA office. A stop at Hans's place brought a minor confrontation with Hans when Dan attempted to cross over the fence after introducing the entourage. "Don't climb through that fence, there is a gate over there and that is what it was made for." The night of the election, everyone was in Wibaux to find out who won the election. Leroy went to sleep in the back seat of the car parked in front of the Sawyer Store. When they all came back, they woke him up and was told of Dan losing the Sheriff's election by only 27 votes. Granddad always said that election outcome was the luckiest day of his life. The war days came bringing better times for farming and ranching. He made more money farming and enjoyed it far more, too. He was losing his farm at Yates and was looking for a way to make a living when he entered the Sheriff's race. Those were tough days.

# COLLEGE:

The NDSL (National Student Defense Loan) program sponsored by the federal government was important for those of us who went on to college by making available monies for our tuition. Pay back was reasonable. Low or no interest was charged. Ten percent payback was required each year for ten years following the first year's grace period. I ended up owing about $1,200 on this program following graduation from Concordia College. Yearly payments of $120 per year were easy to make even though the annual salary of the average graduate at that time was about $5,000. Unfortunately, my sales income was probably around $3,500. The cost of a year's tuition and board at Concordia College was about $1,200 per year. Summer construction jobs and work at the U.S. Dept. of Agriculture's Agricultural Stabilization And Conservation office was important funding my college costs, as was the small amount of money earned shooting jackrabbits during the winter season.

Food around the ranch was pretty cut and dried. Meat and potatoes vegetables and bread. Then this all changed when we went to Fargo/ Moorhead to Concordia College. We learned of pizza. In 1958 the Pizza House medium (10") size pizza having cheese, Italian sausage, pepperoni, anchovy toppings was priced at about $1.75. Later on, there was a new food treat, tacos and tostadas. These cost about fifteen cents each and we devoured them with delight. A year or two later, a new style hamburger place opened. It had golden arches. They sold hamburgers for about fifteen cents, fries about ten cents, and a coke for about twenty-five cents.

One of the cruising destinations was the White Spot, a drive in located about a mile or two south of Concordia College on Hwy 71. Drive-in style food was served and a radio broadcasting station was operated from a shack was installed on the flat roof. It was a swarming place for everyone who had a hot rod to show and sound off.

Choosing my major in college was accomplished at the last minute in my junior year. I chose Economics because it was the class having my highest overall grade point average. Chemistry was chosen as my minor course of study because it was my next highest grade point average. Is this the scientific method or what?

Traveling was always a fun activity I hitched hiked only one time in my career at age 19. I was in Glendive and wanted a ride to Wibaux. I was lucky enough to be picked up by a motorist along US Hwy 10. Times were different in those days. It wasn't so dangerous.

## CELEBRATIONS:

Circuses were held at the ballpark in Wibaux. At one time we were sitting in the stands when the barker asked for volunteers to enter the ring. You guessed it. I was at the head of the line along with Dwayne. We were chosen to join the clowns and animals in the three rings beneath the big top. We were instructed to sit on the circus ring as the clowns were doing their antics as the circus band was playing in the background. Looking out into the crowd and enjoying every minute of our new found fame we basked in the attention and recognition of the townspeople. Our quiet bravado was short lived as the elephants came roaring into the arena behind us. These huge animals trumpeted out the most bloodcurdling noise you ever heard as they quickly moved into the tent. Immediately gone from us for a time was the rapture and mystique of the circus as the crowd roared out in laughter as we jumped up from our places on the ring during this stampede. Its glamour returned shortly after, however, when the clowns appeared and we joined them by participating in their entertainment routine. It was probably then that I decided never run away to join circus. The circus tents were intriguing, the sawdust covered turf along with the animals and performers were wonderful to experience for a fleeting moment at the age of 8 or 10 years. But it was not the lifestyle we wanted. Even so clowning and circus atmospheres have always had an allure since to me to this day.

One of the most memorable Fourth of July celebrations was held at a picnic in the Glendive Park along the Yellowstone River just north of the old iron bridge near downtown Glendive. On the way to the park, a speeding car towing a flatbed trailer piled high with watermelons passed our car. They hit a bump and watermelons rolled off only to be picked up by us as we brought up the rear. They stopped also and it seems as though between us we found one whole melon to be enjoyed later on in the day. We all had a good laugh over this good fortune. It was on this outing that my barefooted brother, Dude, stepped on a barbecue grill at the picnic grounds burning his 4-5 year old tender feet.

It was clown time again during Wibaux's 50th anniversary, Golden Jubilee. Dude, Willie and I had a great time going through the antics of parade clowns. We had two old multicolored cars painted up with polka dots, etc. Dressed in our best clown outfits we performed in the parade. One of our cars had a TV antenna attached. The old vehicles were chugging and smoking along in fine style. Our juggling and clowning around was well received by the crowd. The clown cars were a 1935 Chevrolet Businessman's Coupe and a 1934 Chevrolet four door sedan, as I recall. Driving side by side down the Main Street with long legged Willie Strange astride both vehicles was a sight to behold.

Home coming parades were special each year. Parade floats were constructed on hayracks and were pulled down the street by tractors or trucks. We had an old Model A Ford with a rumble seat that we would take to the homecoming dance. Those who were "fortunate" enough to ride in the rumble seat were treated to high winds and cold temperatures. Inside we all had a great time as they pounded on the car's roof and were shouting out in their chilled condition.

Music Festival in Glendive each year brought out our high school marching band. I played a clarinet and sometimes a bass drum in these festival parades. It was a great experience to step out on the Glendive High School stage with our band to perform for the judges. We always did well. We all were very proud of our group and our music always brought high marks.

We attended school and commercial carnivals on every opportunity. School carnivals were money-raising events that included a number of homemade types of games. One, I especially remember, was a "fishing pole game." A curtain was installed over a corner of the gym behind which were a couple of volunteer operators. Those players who purchased tickets to play and were given a "fishing pole." The line was thrown over the curtain and a prize was attached, a tug was given on the string and the player retrieved a novelty.

Commercial carnivals were presented by traveling groups who would come to town, set up tents, equipment and all of their paraphernalia. A barker using recorded music called people into the area to try their luck at roulette, marksmanship rifle ranges, darts and balloons, ring toss, milk bottle and soft ball toss, to name only a few. Some carnivals had "novelty shows." The adult entertainment girlie sideshows were well attended. The rides were a special treat. The Ferris wheel, kiddie car rides, the tilt-a-whirl, haunted houses, fun houses all made for a great time for old and young alike. Carnivals were present at all Fourth of July celebrations in Glendive & Sidney, and at the ballparks in Wibaux and Beach, ND at other times.

Christmas was a big time for all of us kids. We would try to stay awake to see Santa come with his bag of toys. Somehow we always dozed off and missed seeing him every year. Some of us have, in later years, retained this ability to doze off in church, meetings, and in front of the TV.

Probably one of the memorable gifts I ever received was from Pam. It is a calendar book entitled "Dad, Share your Life With Me." Each day there is a question about my life and a space for an answer. In fact, sections of it have been used as a general outline for this book. "Developing Character Or Creating Characters" should give insights as to our life on the prairie, why we act and do the things we do. It will tell a lot about the family, Eastern Montana residents and myself.

For a few years I was asked to be Santa Claus at the Wibaux Drug during the Christmas season. I remember sitting in the back of the Drug Store surrounded by kids of all ages. They were intent in enumerating their list of wants for Christmas. My costume was not too convincing but I believe that my appearance had little to do with their need to communicate to someone outside of their parents. Believe and maybe it will be so. It was certain that the "elves" were in the wings listening to their requisitions. I wonder where these little kids are today?

Downtown Wibaux was decorated for Christmas. A giant Christmas tree was erected on the corner of Main Street now occupied by the Wibaux County Courthouse. This tree must have been thirty feet tall. It had lights all over it and was the center point of the town well into the New Year. Santa Claus would come to town either on a fire truck or in the back of a hayrack trailer pulled by either horses or a tractor. Santa would hand out sacks containing candy, oranges, apples, and nuts. Sometimes you could see under Santa's beard and we all tried to guess who Santa was. Being observant we all knew that he was not the "real" Santa but we were not discriminating when it came to free candy. Some would request a second bag for "grandma in the car!"

Christmas presents included: .22 caliber rifle, air rifles, bow & arrows, clothes and small toys and games. We all appreciated everything we got even though; the gifts were not always plentiful. These were war years and shortly after. Both WWII and Korea build ups caused a decrease in consumer goods. Candy, sugar, metal, paint, rubber, meat, and a whole host of consumer goods we take for granted today were not to be found. We never were rich. We just made do with what we had.

A present I gave to Dad a dictionary as an assist to improve Dad's vocabulary. Dad would use a lot of big words some of which didn't pertain to the thought being conveyed. He loved the book and we both learned a lot from it. My giving it and his receiving it. Dad was well read and was continually interested in a variety of subjects. He was easy going, considerate and kind.

# CHILDHOOD ADVENTURES:

When the warm summer rains would accumulate at the creek near Granddad Trollope's place, we would go down there to throw dirt lumps, rocks and driftwood into the ponds. After a while we would look closely into the water and see little animal like creatures darting around near the bottom. The bravest of us would reach down to scoop up some of these little fellows and to find that they were pollywogs. Placed in an old fruit jar we would see in time their transformation into frogs.

Trying to be of help on the farm as a toddler, I got an oilcan and began climbing onto a disc harrow. Oil was applied to the sharp blades causing me to slip and slice my right calf from ankle to nearly the knee. Mom bandaged this massive cut up and I was left sitting in the shade along the east side of the house next to my trusty Collie dog, Tippie, as comfort. No stitches, no tetanus shots or professional medical attention was received. The scar remains today. The dog and the pain are gone but the memory lives on.

Our old dog named "Tippie" was our constant companion. He protected us from snakes and would signal to Mom where we kids were located. We had some wild animals as pets, also. These included a pet antelope, pigeons and a barn owl. Regular pets included our cocker spaniel dog, cats, and horses. Being raised on a farm we had lots of pets around. The antelope was brought to us by my Granddad. He had crept up on it, as it lay nestled in the prairie grass and brought it to us for our keeping. We fed it skim milk using a pop bottle with a nipple. One day we let it go and for a couple of years afterward this full grown antelope would come back and stand on the hill looking down on the farmstead early in the morning. Then one morning during hunting season his absence was noticed never to return after that. I often wonder what was on his mind when he looked down on us from his solitary stance on that hill. Did he feel that he was between two worlds? Was he accepted by his own herd?

I remember as a child listening to "Ma Perkins, Boston Blacky, Green Hornet, and The FBI In Peace And War" radio programs that were tuned in on the car radio. At home we had a radio that was powered by a six-volt car battery. Electricity would not arrive in Blue Mountain Country until 1949. It was uncanny that we kids could tell automatically when the programs were to air having no clock or watch to guide us. At the designated time, we would turn on the radio set and await the new episode. I cannot remember much about the programs other than the introductory music, the announcer and familiar voices. These like so many of our memories have grown dim and have vanished from the dial only to reappear on our computers in family featured old time radio websites.

Stunts, adventures, and explorations could very well fill another volume. As we go along I will inject some of them to liven up the text as necessary. We used to smoke Indian tobacco down at the creek. This plant grows in wet areas and attains a height of about three feet. It is characterized by a long clump of brown seeds that we thought would be a fine smoking material. We soon found out that when it was rolled into a cylinder and ignited the vapors, smoke and whatever was very hot and caustic. This was awful stuff and it is not recommended for anything other than eradication. It did serve one good purpose, though. It kept me off tobacco until college days.

Kite flying was a diversion also. We had a few kites. We would buy them for twenty-five cents to fifty cents over at the Variety Store. A ball of string was also added to the purchase. Many times the kites didn't fly. No wind, poor construction or lack of piloting skill was to blame. Other times they flew well. We had a neighbor boy whose kite went hundreds of feet into the air.

Best hide and seek places were found in the hay mow, hay stack, threshing machines, woods, trees, and in barns. We would build hiding places in hay bales and behind tools and equipment. Hiding in the threshing machine was most effective. Whenever hiding, silence and quiet were paramount. It was difficult to stop giggling and laughing while observing how the others conducted their search. As a result, we usually gave ourselves away and were located in those games.

There were a number of nick names that were associated with our friends: Green, Happy Jack, Barney, Rab, Brink, Dude, Rainy, Insky, Grizzly, Princess, and Old Thomse. Never could understand where all of the monikers came from. Just as well in some cases, I expect. It would appear that this added to the informality of growing up at home and in school.

Pranks were a way of having fun. There were so many that it would be difficult to tell them all. Most all of the stunts were not destructive or mean while some were borderline. One time we dug a hole in the unlighted path to the bunkhouse. Having no light the hired man could not see the hole that had been filled with mud. He stepped into this mess on the way to his bunk after a hard day of work. A loud noise was heard which included yelling and maybe even some cussing. That was about the last of our pranks for a longtime. Lucky we didn't get into big trouble on this venture.

Games we used to play included the usual cops and robbers, cowboys and Indians, hide and seek. After a while work became a game to us all. Hauling hay bales, branding cattle, harvesting grain all were games to us as we grew up. Is this a definition of work ethic, work attitudes or a lack of entertainment choices? We learned that if everybody did their chores we all would eat well and the family would greatly benefit.

One of the most intriguing games that we would play was a puppet game in which one child would get under a bed, extend his arms and hands. Another child would tie a handkerchief around the doubled up fists and a face was drawn on the cloth. Then the little kids would be brought into the room to talk to this puppet. It was quite realistic and I still can visualize this game. Creativity was a must because we did not have toys or electronic games to play. We had to make do with what was available. "Plowing" in the dirt using Mom's kitchen serving spoons and blowing bubbles using a spool, soap and water were some of the activities we had. Making willow whistles from tree limbs and bows and arrows from the ash tree branches was a fun diversion. Bean shooters were made from clothespins. Whistles were made from blades of grass. Two tin cans, brown wrapping paper and string were fashioned into a working "telephone." Firecracker guns were made out of galvanized pipes that used firecrackers and bolts for ammo. Rubber band guns were carved and were fitted with clothespins to provide a trigger to launch rubber bands cut from old tire inner tubes.

Fourth of July was a great time. It brought fireworks and the fun that we had with them. Firecrackers, Roman candles, "snakes", and pop bottle rockets were our favorites. We would invert a tin can over a firecracker before igniting it causing the can to fly high into the sky. One stunt that backfired, literally, was smoking unexploded firecrackers. These were lit and placed in the mouth like cigarettes. Worked fine until one blew up in my mouth. Purple lips adorned my countenance for a while after that misadventure. Fourth of July celebrations included attending rodeos and stage shows at the county fair grounds in Glendive and Sidney, Montana. Acrobats, trained dogs, dancers, comedians, live bands and the action of the rodeo were immensely entertaining. Fireworks were displayed following the main show. Eating cotton candy and drinking soda pop made the outing a big time event that will never be forgotten.

To escape summer heat one of the cool places where we would play was in the dirt basement of our farmhouse. Of great interest to us there were the toads that lived in the cool, moist soil. We would pick them up and carry them around, as I recall. Later I got warts all over my hands from this exposure evidently due to the virus containing liquids on this reptile's skin. See that's what you get when you play with toads. Multiple warts grew and the only remedy offered was an old wife's tale that the cure to be effected required burying Mom's kitchen dishcloth. This was said to banish the curse of warts. A dishrag was surreptitiously removed from the kitchen, taken to the north side of the house's foundation, and was buried. You know, it did work. All warts except one left my hands. That one was picked off during school classroom hours. With technology another "cure" has bit the dust all because of automatic dishwashers.

We all enjoyed the outdoors. The wide open outdoors was so important to us as we were growing up. Fresh air, flowing streams, prairies, and woods gave us freedom and independence. There were only distant neighbors. The value of wide-open spaces is not readily be understood by many townsmen or even politicians. Rambling walks along Beaver Creek, exploring the bluffs north of town, vacant buildings, rummaging around the junkyard and walks in the pastures and wooded draws were some of the places of meditation, contemplation and adventure. We grew up like Tom Sawyer and Huckleberry Finn with whom we readily identified.

One time while camping along Beaver Creek in Wibaux, we built a fire, told stories and ate food we packed in. Unfortunately, to mar the occasion, when settling down for the night we ended up burning a hole in Jim's expensive sleeping bag. Sleeping out in the open air was a wondrous experience. We could see millions of stars on a clear night. Montana is a place where you can see forever and where you can hear quiet.

As a youngster I remember looking up in the sky seeing an unusual cloud. After gazing at it for a period of time, various shapes were observed. At that time there was a feeling of peace and contentment and a sense of God's presence that I have never felt to the same degree since. Even today, I think of that time as I travel past that hill and search the sky above. "I will lift up mine eyes unto the hills, from whence cometh my help."

Later on in life, I still believed that there was a pot of gold at the end of the rainbow. We never did find that pot of gold but the rain that preceded it was better than any old yellow metal that we could ever venture to come upon. Clean, fresh air and water for the crops was all we needed. Although the Assurance from Above was always appreciated.

Probably the neatest time we ever had on the ranch was springtime. After the long cold winters the sun would melt the snow and little creeks of flowing water were everywhere. Meadowlarks would sit on fence posts and their songs were the most beautiful music I have ever heard. In the pastures crocus and gumbo lilies would blossom. Baby calves, chicks, foals and lambs would appear all over the landscape. These were the signs of reawakening and new beginnings. To me it was a glimpse of heaven to see this rebirth after the long cold winter.

Holidays and family get togethers were wonderful times because the whole family including cousins, aunts, uncles, grand parents met for fun, food, discussion and games. The importance of family was one of the values that we learned in this rural country setting. Church was always a major emphasis in our family's life. Every New Years & Christmas church services included candlelight observances, Christmas trees, candy, gifts; singing and a special glow surrounded all of these activities. New Year's Day was involved a family get together with the cousins, aunts, uncles, grandparents, and sometimes a friend of the family or two. Feasts, games, and discussions prevailed all day. If the house was too small, then the children usually went outside to hunt rabbits, sled on the hills, or skate on the dam or creek. New Year's Eve celebrations included church services with parties afterwards.

Special exploring places for us were the bluffs along Beaver Creek north of the highway bridge in Wibaux. Trees and draws on the ranch provided our own territory to be investigated. Caves we built by digging up the sod always spurred our imagination. Rafts and tree houses were all great places for us live out our adventures. We climbed under buildings, scaled trees, crawled under railroad and highway bridges, rode horses and bicycles. Ice-skating. Summer or winter we were outside much of the time. We learned to love the open air, sky, clouds, grass, trees, and streams.

We enjoyed making mud pies. We would sit in the shade during the summer (no air conditioning . . . no electricity for many years) making mud pies. I expect that there times when we threw the mud in mud fights, too. No politics there!

Summertime brought a time of freedom and independence on the ranch. Growing up in this atmosphere was wonderful giving us a love of the outdoors, growing things, people, and work around the farmstead. While it was hot and dry most of the time we hardly ever went barefoot. Grass, stones, snakes, and sharp stubble was not welcoming to our tender feet.

Being boys, we spent a lot of time hanging hand over hand in acrobatics overhead in the barn, burrowing into stored grain in the bins, jumping on the haystacks, hiding in combines and old threshing machines, throwing rocks and dirt lumps, making bows and arrows, raiding birds nests, fishing with yarn and bobby pin tackle, shooting BB guns, playing cowboys and Indians, going on adventures, riding bicycles, building forts in ice and snow, playing hide and seek, wrestling and fighting, building campfires, sleeping out at night, hiking, riding horses, swimming in the dam, riding horses, building rafts and tree houses, reading comic books, constructing firecracker guns and enjoying the noise that our "Black

Cat" and "Lady Fingers" crackers would emit around the fourth of July. Each summer day was enjoyed to its fullest knowing that time was fleeting and we would soon be back to boring classrooms joining our friends with whom we could share our summer exploits.

Three brothers aged one year apart, we were constantly getting into one scrape or another. Exploring ponds, creeks, bluffs; burning coalmines, and especially climbing under the railroad and highway bridges were antics that our parents really never knew about. Climbing under the bridges while standing on narrow bridge "I" beams in snow and cold has got to be one of the most dangerous stunts we pulled. I remember one time we were half way across the railroad bridge over Beaver Creek when a freight train passed overhead. A fall of about 30 feet into the creek below was the least that could have happened with just one slip. Looking upwards to view the underbellies of the freight cars hell-bent for Minneapolis and to hear the thunderous noise just a few feet above us was thrilling. Building rafts and floating on ponds while playing pirates was an activity engaged in on Beaver Creek. Sometimes we would use big blocks of ice as rafts on swollen creeks for especially exciting times. Our tree house construction and clubhouse activities of burning kerosene lamps and imagining attacking Indians or other warriors were common diversions. We literally lived the life of "Tom Sawyer & Huckleberry Finn".

Hot summer days would find us kids playing in the stock water tank, in a cool root cellar, digging a cave in the woods, playing in the shade and probably drinking a Kool-Aid type of drink. The drink was formulated using a bottle of flavoring mixed with sugar and ice water to provide a much sought after refreshment. "Don't go outside without your hat" was a theme we heard frequently from Mom. We all wore shoes because of the hot sod and stubble of the yard. We all wore overalls, cotton T-shirts, socks and shoes. There were times when the shirts were discarded in favor of a great suntan. Working on rooftops and in the direct sunshine during roof repair raised sunburn blisters that I will not soon forget. I remember one time, especially, in which huge blisters were raised on our backs and there was little that could be done to relieve the pain and ensure proper healing. Sometimes, cow's cream was smoothed on the burns. Usually, though in a day or two the blisters would break leaving a scaly skin that shed like a snake's hide. This condition was exceeding uncomfortable as the healing process progressed.

Some of the make believe games and activities included pretending that we were explorers, climbing bluffs, rafting on the creek, camping out. Cops and robbers/ cowboys and Indians were fun times. We would play hide and seek also. We got so good at this activity that it wasn't fun any more because we could never find each other.

Growing up in small town Wibaux we never cussed at all, played hooky and we never called in sick at school. Telling the truth was high on everyone's list. Now that is not to say that we were angels because we weren't. But there are not any times that I could remember in which we could be blamed for major lying or cussing. If we did, we would be reported to our parents by teachers, pastors, relatives, and others. "Takes a village to raise a kid." I have added to this slogan, "It takes 40 acres to raise a kid."

Leisure activities included hunting, fishing, hiking, exploring, board games, sledding, skiing, hauling hay, feeding cattle, farm chores were super activities that assured that we were adequately entertained. There was no TV and no radio that worked well.

While in Wibaux or Glendive we visited various stores and poring over merchandise that we had never seen before. Woolworth Five & Dime Store, Dry Goods Store, Variety Store, Drug Store, and Hardware Stores were our favorite haunts. We looked over comic books, toys, games, bicycles, scooters, jackknives, and air rifles. There were precious few times that our pockets ever had a quarter or a half dollar so purchasing items was a rarity. The most memorable gift I gave to my mom was two paring knives that I bought in 1946 at Hiles Dry Goods Store on Main Street where now is located the

Shamrock Restaurant/Bar. I paid 25 cents for the two of them. They had red painted wooden handles.

Some of the ingenious engineering projects we constructed included bow and arrows, tree houses, caves in the ground, forts in the snow, rafts on the swollen creek, firecracker guns, bean shooters, and a radio that broadcasted all over town our version of music for all ages.

Being afraid of getting lost in a big town was always of concern to us kids. Glendive, Montana was a big town. We always stayed close to the folks when we traveled to that place. At the age of about four years, I would hold onto my mom's dress as she went from store to store. We all were a bit shy in those days. We just were not accustomed to being around people. You might have called us "backward." Most all of us country kids had that complex. Some really never overcame it. Then there were some who just used this complex as a springboard to more extroverted behavior. Katy bar the door!

There were a lot of celebrations during the year. May baskets delivered to our cousins were memorable. We would make May baskets and drop them off at their houses. They would try to catch us after we left them on their doorsteps, knocked on the door and ran. They would catch us and give us a kiss and a big hug when we got caught. The May baskets were made of Dixie paper cups having pipe stem handles being decorated with ribbons and colored paper. They were filled with some small bits of candy.

When we went to town we would buy ice cream cones for five and ten cents-single dip & double dip. Do you suppose that is where the term, "double dip," came from? A glass of Coke would also cost five or ten cents. A comic book cost ten cents. All were purchased at the drug store.

Uncle Rueben and his twin brother Roy had their farms nearby in the Cottonwood Community. Reuben would take us out on his farm/ranch to check on his sheep in the outback. We would ride along with the pickup truck's radio blaring "Back To The Bible" with the program's stories & songs. In later years, it was Reuben who was helpful in steering me to a job with the Agricultural Stabilization and Conservation office in Wibaux without which I could not have gone to college. Roy was a farmer and in the early years was a schoolteacher at the nearby Williams School, which was located on the hill south of his farmstead. Roy would tell stories and joke with us kids. Both Uncles had infectious laughs and great senses of humor.

All of our uncles and aunts were our "favorites." It was from them that we learned how to share stories and events from which we could all benefit.

One of the best tree houses we constructed was in the upper reaches of a tall cottonwood tree along the levee near the railroad bridge. It was fully enclosed and we had an old kerosene lantern inside for heat and light. Calvin and I built it. One other tree house was on the farm. It wasn't too high in the old elm tree near the water well east of the house. These "club houses" gave us fellows a place to meet and discuss the affairs of the day and to plan our next adventure.

There was only one place for our recreation in downtown Wibaux. It was located in the recreation room in the basement of the Drug Store. It had a pool table, soda fountain, board games, comics etc. This was a great hang out for us all.

We used to go the high school gym after hours also to play basketball. Getting into the gym was easy, just climb onto the window ledges on the north side of the building, lift the metal-framed windows and crawl through the crack, dropping to the gym floor below. There were some kids who probably entered the building using this method of entry more times than they did using the front door.

Our cousins were like brothers and sisters to us all. There were about fifteen of us and we all got together at holiday times, especially. I remember Arla had pure white, long hair, which took a long time to dry after shampooing. One day I threw a dirt lump at her after she had spent much time drying her wet hair. It hit her in the head necessitating a return to the kitchen where the process of washing and drying had to be repeated. No hair dryers in those days. Lots of dirt lumps, though.

Riding in cousin's Ronald, Marlene, and Norrine pony drawn wagon was fun. Ronald also made a motorized cart out of Maytag washing machine motor, four wagon wheels, a six foot length of 2"X12" plank and some rope. It went down hill in good fashion but not uphill. That old Maytag engine vibrated, smoked, and made its peculiar noise. Steering was accomplished by pulling on two ropes attached to the front wheel axle.

Music was important. Christmas songs were especially remembered. "Here Comes Santa Claus" sung by Gene Autry. "Frosty The Snowman", "Rudolph The Red Nose Reindeer". Christmas Carols. These were the most memorable. Oh, don't forget Hank Williams, country western tunes and most all of the Hee Haw barn dance performers on TV.

In the 1950's, rock and roll music took over. Popular songs of the day included: "Green Door", "You Ain't Nothin' But A Hound Dog", "Jail House Rock", and "Surfer Joe". Elvis Presley, Bill Haley and the Comets, Jim Lowe, George Hamilton The Fourth, Eddy Arnold, Lawrence Welk, Tennessee Ernie Ford, Vic Damone, Richy Valens, Buddy Holly, The Big Bopper, Four Freshmen were some of the great entertainers we enjoyed. Probably the most sung song by us kids was the novelty song, "One Eyed Flying Purple People Eater" by Ray Stevens.

Favorite dances included: The Butter Fly Dance, Square Dances, Ball Room Dances and the Twist. I never was much of a dancer. Just couldn't seem to get the hang of it. Liked the music though. We all enjoyed going to dances. Walking and chewing gum was a real task for us coordination challenged boys. But give us a basketball or football and we could run circles around anything on the floor or the field. Dancing was another subject all together.

About the first formal dance we attended was the Rainbow Girls Christmas Formal Dance in Beach, ND in about 1957. We all had dates and went to the dance at the lodge hall. Can't remember much about it though. Seems as though there were awards and recognition ceremonies or something. We guys weren't tuned into the program, as I recall. But in spite of the decorations, music, food, and laughter we still would rather have been out hunting rabbits.

Now high school Junior Prom & Senior Proms was another story. Coats, shirts & ties were in order. Corsages and boutonnieres were worn. The gymnasium was fantastically decorated and excellent live music was present. A grand parade of all the participants was a part of the evening's festivities. This was always a top-drawer event. Filling out dance cards was the order of the night.

The subject of discipline in the family was important because we were crowded together in a very small house. We needed to pay attention to the tasks at hand. We did not have much time for foolishness or fighting. Sounds good, doesn't it. Well there were times when we were spanked using bare hand or sometimes a stick was added to make the experience even more memorable. Mostly, for unruly behavior, discipline took the form of sitting in a chair and being quiet. That is a tough punishment when everyone else is rollicking in the freedom of the great outdoors. Some of the discipline may sound barbaric today but it was quite common in every household in our time. "Spare the rod and spoil the child" just had to be true, right?

Not that we didn't deserve the punishment we got. Three boys all about the same age was a recipe for occasional conflict, if not all out war. One time one of us hit the other over the head with a hoe. One other time I unintentionally threw red pepper in my brother's eyes as we were exiting the root cellar under the house. Then there were the dirt fights; firecracker attacks, wrestling matches, and general roughhousing that took place. Unfortunately, we were usually caught and all suffered punishment of one kind or another.

Imaginary friends are sometimes a part of growing up. I can't remember if we had any. But if we did, it had to be "Brink". While playing war, cops & robbers or cowboys & Indians we all wanted to be our hero, "Brink". We never could figure out where that name came from or why "he" was so popular with us.

Most of us have few mementos of the early years. One item, I have is a baby shoe with barnyard manure still on it. Don't know what happened to the other shoe. Guess that I am waiting for it to drop or maybe it already has dropped into a place that is inaccessible.

Superstitions were always present when we were young. We were afraid of ghosts on the farm because of the lack of nightlights and the ever-present concern over the dark. One thing that ranch life offered was darkness with murkiness due to a lack of electric lights. On dark nights buildings sometimes became foreboding and we would think that we saw ghosts, monsters under the bed, and various apparitions, etc. Some of the places still hold a certain amount of mystery to me after all of these years.

Weather out on the plains is unpredictable. Temperatures during the winter of 1949 plunged to minus 50 degrees at night and minus 25 degrees during the daytime. We got a lot of snow. Roads were blocked and almost all activity ceased. Government Caterpillar tractors eventually came in to plow snow and ice. U.S. military planes airlifted hay to stranded cattle isolated in rural pastures. Cold temperatures remained for a week. The frost-encrusted hinges on doors would scream out when the door was opened. Residents fought deep snow for up to three weeks being stranded in their ranch houses unable to reach town. They lived off produce from their ranches. Eggs, milk, and butchered meat plus whatever they had in their root cellars and canned goods in their pantries kept them alive.

Snow brought us fun outside. We had Flexible Flyer sleds and old wooden skis. Sleds would travel very fast. We would slide down a hill and fly over a stretch of open water on the creek. Each time breaking off more ice in the creek bed until we ended up kerplop in the water 6"-10" deep. Other times we would slide down hill on city streets, and sidewalks near the schoolhouse in town. We spent much time outside because our house was small. No TV. No radio.

Playing in the snow was great fun. Building snow forts, digging caves, and building snowmen seemed to be a never-ending activity. Our snowmen were a bit unusual. They didn't have faces. No coal or carrots were available to provide the familiar features found on most snowmen of the day.

One time while exploring along Beaver Creek I found two Black Birds or Grackles that had fallen from the railroad bridge during a wet, cold snowstorm. Both birds were near death. I took them to our cave and stoked up a fire consisting of leaves, paper, and sticks. The birds were placed near the fire for warming. As they lay there their feathers began steaming as they began to dry out. One of the birds revived and jumped into the fire while the other bird remained motionless at the side of the fire. In the end, the bird that flew into the fire lived and the other bird died. This object lesson has been with me ever since. Get involved. React. Take charge. Fly into the fire.

Rickey and I hunted rabbits at during cold winter nights, operated a wireless radio station and began a rocketry project in high school. We do not mention here my abominable win-loss record at chess and Parcheesi.

The first bicycle I ever had was an old bike that Granddad John allowed us to ride. It was way too large for me. I could hardly reach the pedals. I leaned the bike against an old horse drawn grain wagon on the hill near their ranch house, hopped aboard the two wheeler and rode it through the farm yard until it fell over. Then back to the wagon for another try. After several tries, somehow, I could ride it rather decently. Needless to say, like most things in later life, we learned by trial and error or by accident.

Ice-skating was a big activity for us. Grandfather Dan gave me a pair of skates, which I still have. These skates opened up a brand new reason to be out on the ice in the cold and allowed me to join the other kids in their skating parties and fun. There were warm up shelters on the flooded ice rink near the school. On other occasions when skating on the creek we would burn old tires and logs to keep warm. We had skating parties at school and church. Our town would flood a skating rink and there was always the farm pond, dam, and Beaver Creek to provide plenty of icy fun. We would skate into the evening hours beneath the full moon and stars. These were very memorable times. Hot chocolate-cookies-candy-popcorn was served sometimes as we rallied around the fires.

Winter still is one of my favorite times of the year.

Some of my friends had things that I did not have. But I had things that they didn't have so there was not a serious case of envy anywhere. It is a bit unnerving now to think of how little we all had and yet there were no real hardships. There was one area of contention, however. That was the clubhouse, which a friend had, and he would not let the rest of us inside to see it. It was very fancy. Funny, that clubhouse was located next to a big cottonwood tree in what is now my mother's yard. Clubhouse is gone. Friend is gone. Families are gone. The only thing left is that old tree. Goes to show how those things we think are so important are only temporary and how you might not get to go into the clubhouse but some day you might own it, the trees, and the house to go with it. Kind of like the story of a rich business leader in town during the 1940's who came up to one of our relatives and said, "When I get to be tail twister of Wibaux County, this is the way that it's going to be . . ." It was some years later, he became powerful and had a lot of control in the county, however his health was failing and it was all for naught. Power and wealth are all transitory. His memory has faded from the county and the power he had has evaporated.

New Year's Resolutions were not a big deal in our town. Hoping and praying for better times we just wanted to continue doing what we did best—survive.

# CARS:

The first car that I owned outright was a 1951 Chevrolet that I bought for $13.00. It had no reverse gear allowing for forward movement only. A Concordia College classmate had an old green car parked in his dad's driveway for weeks. His dad finally gave him orders to get rid of it. I was the lucky winner and found that the car was very serviceable having driven it for a couple of years prior to having it accidentally burned up by a discarded cigarette some years later. The longest single trip made with it was from Fargo-Moorhead to its final home in Wibaux. I learned that reverse gear was not that important. All you needed to do was to park where you weren't required to back up. Maybe this old car had more affect on me in later years than anything I learned in school. Full steam ahead. Don't look back.

My second car was another 1951-52 Chevrolet I drove while working for the ASC agricultural office during the summers. Good old car but it did burn a little oil. Gasoline probably was about 30 cents per gallon. A quart of oil was about fifty cents. Tires were about $20.00 each. Most generally the top speed this car was driven was less than 50MPH. Most generally we cruised around at about 35MPH. One summer day I had an interesting accident with that Chevy while at work. Driving north of town along Beaver Creek on my way to see a farmer, I drove up to his gate. No brakes. The car smashed right through that old board fence and gate. Needless to say, I felt very bad about this but the farmer took it in good humor. Another time

I took a short cut down a heavily grassed farm lane only to find that it was a regular slough due to recent rainstorms. The car traveled about 50 yards into the "swamp" and came to rest. A farmer had to pull it out with his tractor.

My next car cost $150.00. It was a 1949 Dodge that I bought from Hammond Implement. Funny thing this car had both an automatic and stick shift feature. You could shift the gears manually or merely shift into "drive" and the shifting was automatic. This car was driven to St. Paul, MN and later to Madison, WI when I took my first job with Monroe Calculators. That old gray monster had a six-cylinder engine that was so cold blooded it did not start well in cold Wisconsin winters. It was sold to a used car dealer for $25.00 after receiving complaints from my landlady that the heap was parked out front on the city street too long. Later while in Wibaux I got a call from Hammond Implement advising that I had not paid my last car payment in the amount of fifteen dollars. Evidently, they had not deposited my check before I closed out my St. Paul, MN bank account. I had to fork over the $15.00 due them to clear their books. Can anybody imagine a salesman driving a 13-year-old car with Montana license plates making sales calls all over the St. Paul and Madison areas? In real estate they say "Location, Location, Location" is needed for success. How about "Perception, Perception, Perception" is needed for success in business. These obstacles were overcome with no small amount of difficulty as things go better and better.

My next car was a 1956 Chevrolet, which was purchased for $300.00. It was not in the best of shape either. Dad & I did some work on it before my trek back to Madison, WI. I drove it for a year or so making sales calls in SW Wisconsin. Then one day just south of New Glarus, WI. the motor made a loud noise and smoke rose from the tailpipe. The motor blew a piston. The car was towed into the shop and I managed to get back to Madison somehow. A visit to the Montgomery Ward store resulted in the purchase of a rebuilt motor block. It was delivered directly to the New Glarus shop and in a day or two it was back on the road. Of course, I had to borrow money, about $350.00 as I recall, to pay for the work done. No credit cards. No credit. I went to a small loan company and they granted a loan at about 25% interest. Monthly payments were about $25.00 per month. I paid on this loan for about three or four years before it was paid it off in a lump sum amounting to about $150.00. Learning high finance and high interest rates is a painful experience.

The old '56 Chevrolet needed to be replaced. The bank in Wibaux was quick to oblige me in a trade for a 1963 Chevrolet, which was traded in later for a 1967 Ford Fairlane.

# WHO AM I?

My name, Loraine Dennis Trollope, was never chosen for any special reason other than what I learned in later life. Dad spent time with a friend whose name of was Loraine in the late 1930's at a Civilian Conservation Corps near Bozeman, MT. I spelled this moniker with two "R's" for about 38 years or so until one day I looked at my birth certificate and found that the correct spelling has only one "R" in it. Grandma Alberta Trollope for years contended that I had spelled it wrong all through school. You know, she was right. My lack of attention to detail was obscured by my inability to heed advice???

Some have asked what was my best talent. Hard to say. I guess humor and hard work would be on the list. Early on, it was obvious that speech was high on my talent inventory. Communicating in all situations was a real gift. Management ranked lower on my skills evaluation portfolio but there were times when I was thrust into situations that required managing people. In management venues, my greatest fault was that of impatience and thinking too far ahead of the group. Visionary or forward thinking has good outcomes most times. The downside was the cost of staff attrition and inefficiency if the group was not inclined to change or had an uncommitted attitude concerning the goals and objectives to be achieved.

# JOB HUNTING:

After graduating from Concordia College with a Major in Economics and a Minor in Chemistry, it became important to put this good knowledge to work to pay off the accumulated outstanding $1,200 educational loan. An appointment for a job interview was made with the bank in Helena, MT. Mom, Adele and I traveled from Wibaux to Helena for this first job opportunity. Before we left, we filled (3) five-gallon cans of gasoline, placing them in the car's trunk to fuel our way out west. There was not enough money for store bought gasoline. We arrived at the bank, met an officer, completed a short interview, packed up and left. No job offer. No thanks.

After traveling to Minneapolis on a Greyhound Bus my next job interview was at a stock brokerage house. This resulted in a fancy lunch and little else. No job offer. No thanks.

Next scheduled job interview was with a large downtown Minneapolis bank. I strode into the manager's office and was seated in a diminutive position across from this huge desk. On the other side of the desk was seated a rather pompous individual dressed in a suit and tie. He asked why I was there and I reminded him of our job interview appointment. He laughed and was visibly shaken with what appeared to him to be a hilarious response. He said that the position was that of a bill collector for the Southside of Minneapolis and that if the bank hired me for that position area residents would run me out of the neighborhood. No further discussion. No job offer. No thanks.

Readers can deduce by this time that my enthusiasm for the big city was waning. But on with the program by appearing at my next interview with an agricultural products processor located in a tall building in downtown St. Paul, Minnesota. Arriving early for the appointment and needing a rest, I stopped by a nearby office whose door was open, entered and promptly was seated on their fine sofa in the waiting room. An attendant came by and stated that they were an employment agency and that if I would complete the form, they would seek a job for me at a cost of about $400. For the first time in weeks, there was an individual pledged to help me. Upon completion of the employment contract application, I took the elevator up to meet with the agricultural processing company. They were advertising for help in their human resources department. True to form, this encounter resulted in another rather quick interview having no real depth or substance. No job offer. No thanks.

By now, I was becoming discouraged and angered in this employment search. It was my understanding that a person with a college degree was assured employment. Not so. I felt that the system had lied to me. With a feeling of frustration and distaste for the system, I boarded the city bus that would take me back across town to my room at Anderson Hotel in downtown Minneapolis. As I walked into the lobby area, someone behind the desk called out my name stating that I had a message. Hearing my name voiced in any Minneapolis venue was a startling event for me. Feeling like a celebrity after the reception I had received from previous appointments and interviews that had failed to produce any acknowledgement at all, this summons seemed like a miracle. The handwritten message was from the employment agency informing me of a job interview that they had set up for me for the next morning with Monroe Calculator Company on Roberts Street in downtown St. Paul. Taking an early city bus across Minneapolis to St. Paul, I showed up on time, was ushered into the sales manager's office and told that the manager would be in to see me momentarily. Being somewhat nonplused, frustrated and disgruntled, I seated myself in his chair behind the desk. He came in and asked if my name was Loraine Trollope and I responded by saying that it indeed was my name. In a tone of voice that could almost be misconstrued as a warning, I told him I had been in his office only a minute or two and I already had his desk. Then realizing the possible gravity of this mistaken retort, the return of his desk was offered. He declined saying stay where you are, that he would sit in the chair on the other side of the desk. After a short chitchat he asked when I could start work. July 5, 1962 was the answer I gave. I found out later that every salesman that he had on staff was as brash as I was in this brief interview. His assembled team was of the same aggressive mind. Maybe there was some modicum of promise in this business world after all! Job found.

Special Note: These job interview and search descriptions were held at a time during the worst downturn in the economy since the 1929 Stock Market Crash. Poor economic conditions and dismal future outlook were major factors in the lack of my early success in obtaining employment. Of course, my interviewing skills had not been developed as yet, either. Having no advance personal referrals, references or resume' could have been a part of the problem also. Adverse employment prospects were revealed earlier and they should have given indication as to the job market when after sending out about 70 letters addressing advertised positions only about three or four responses were even acknowledged and these were all negative. Tough times experienced on the farm translated into tough times in the city. Being met with negativity only seemed to build my resolve to continue to fight for a position in the workplace to prove my worth. As it turned out after studying diligently and observing successful salesmen at work, I made several large, unexpected sales of equipment and later went on to be the leading sales trainee west of the Mississippi River. In a few months I became, I believe, the youngest trainer of marketing personnel in the company having been instrumental in hiring and training the salesman who became the national director of sales in the New Jersey Home Office. All of this was accomplished before the age of 25 years. This paragraph is not added for bravado, far be it. The purpose is to relate my perspective of what takes place in Montanans who are met with limited opportunity but respond with their unstoppable "can do" attitude. To me this is what this book is all about. Some would say that it is something in the water that promotes the fierce desire to succeed. Others would say that it is just a response of growing up in an environment of diversity and scarcity that builds character. Would we want it to be any different?

# A COWPOKE STORY

By: Stanley Arden Trollope

Written In
Early 1960's

## Page 1

Charlie really didn't care, suppose because of his earlier background, that he was the one to have to do the milking on Sunday morning. The one thing that puzzled him was his two pals who bunked with him in the bunkhouse on the (Circle S). The fact that Joe Carney and Chris Olson always rode in about three or four o'clock Sunday mornings after a night in town singing and happy, and the fact that dynamite couldn't blow them out of bed after they went to sleep. It had never occurred to Charlie that it could have been the moonshine in them, the only thing he knew about that was what he had heard from Chuck Grant, and the fellow that had raised him on a ranch South of Medora.

Charley's early life was sketchy as some said he was the only survivor of a stage holdup that ran south of Medora to North Platte, Nebraska.

At any rate he would up at Chuck Grant's spread at the age of two. Golly, that didn't seem like fifteen years ago. Much had happened

Page 2
To little Charlie as he was affectionately called by Mr. Grant's hands who had taught him the folklore of the West, how to read and write, use a gun and straddle a wild bronco. All of which, Charlie could do with equal ease and remarkably well.

Charlie looked and dressed like any other young cowboy of his time except for the derby hat that "Silver John" Clay gave him on one of his silver mine stock selling sprees, which he took frequently among the rich ranchers of the West. Silver John took a real liking to Charlie and gave him a derby hat, which Charlie cherished greatly, and was never without it.

The hat was the butt of many jokes and dealt poor Charlie with much ridicule and good-natured laughter, but he never parted with it.

His early life was much the same as any young boy's of his time, he learned to stay clear of trouble, particularly the rampaging Sioux Indians that were very difficult to get along with because of the slaughter of the wild game that had been their food and means of life for so long.

Page 3
Charlie got to know quite a few of them around Medora and Mingusville. He probably thought it would be to his advantage as he was quite fond of his dark curly hair.

He knew the three great Chiefs the one to the North, the one to the South, and also Chief "Fox Eyes" to the West. It was rather odd how he had become friends with Fox Eyes. The Old Indian couldn't understand how the blue coat soldiers could transmit messages so quickly from Sentinel Butte to Pompey's Pillar. So Charlie had explained that they could dot and dash messages with a mirror from station to station some thirty to sixty miles apart. Fox Eyes probably didn't believe him but at least he felt that he had a white ally.

The fact that he was more or less free from Indian danger and could travel freely about hunting probably brought the writing of the story to follow.

Page 4
On one of Charlie's hunting trips he happened across a horse camp of Walt Ryan's who happened to be hiring hands, the pay was $15 per month and board which was the first money he had ever earned. His job was to wrangle the remuda or working saddle horses as we call them now days. He never even bothered to go back to tell the Grant's where he was going, OK don't misunderstand he always intended to but some how the years slipped by and he didn't for many years to come. To become a full time hand at the age of 13 was quite a task for a boy. The work wasn't so bad but that infernal gathering of firewood, which he kept tied to the rear of the chuck wagon with a rope.

Charlie couldn't never quite understand how his crew "acquired" the horses that they were to deliver to Fort Keogh at Miles City. All he knew was that the herd kept getting larger and larger. He also thought that Captain Miles must be a very rich man to pay for the well over a thousand head of good horses at one time.

Page 5

All went well for the crew until the fording of the Yellowstone River. Charlie was just plain scared. He had heard much from old timers about the sand holes and pockets in the Yellowstone River until he felt as though he should like to be in the safe confines of Mr. Grant's care once more.

There was a landing pier at Glenvale or Glendale or something like that and that was where they were supposed to cross. But being June the badlands creek to the south was badly swollen so they had to swing far to the north then back. This was the first time since early March that any of the cowboys had seen a woman. There were quite a few on the flat bottom paddle wheeler that was moored at the dock in Glendale. They were busy unloading supplies and on the return trip would haul some of the great woolsacks that had come in from the range wagons hauling from around Miles City. There was great excitement among the people as they saw the great migration of buffalo that swam the river headed, it seemed to Charlie, in a northwesterly direction. There were a large number; some old timers said there was around 15-20 thousand in the bunch. And when they moved though slowly the dust would almost blot out the sun. The stragglers that followed the herd were being barked at by the Indian dogs of the friendly Cheyenne that were camped among the cottonwoods along the Yellowstone. Some brave hearted young Indian occasionally would bring in a buffalo calf, which was eaten at once amid much rejoicing.

However, Charlie was more interested in one of the riverboat captain's lovely daughters, who he was to meet and court in his later years. She even gave him a piece of black silk which he tied around his neck as a "tough rag" and he left it there for many years until it was a little more than a string. It was real handy for him to slip up over his nose when it was real dusty, and helped him to breath. Also the black went well with his black derby.

**Page 6**
It sure looked like there wouldn't be any $500 bonus for the delivery of the horses, but I am getting ahead of the story. Because it was Monday night, after all the boys had spent the weekend at the Glendale shipping wharf, and the fact that Charlie had become a first class wrangler probably was the reason he was the only man on guard that night. Coupled with the fact that most of the horses now numbering around 750 in all were tired and many were sleeping on their feet. Also, Mr. Groves had selected a large grassy canyon for the night stop making it very easy to watch the bunch. Charlie rode up on a knoll by the twisted old cedar clump where he could have a good vantage point to see everything. The first part of the evening was broken only by the who-who of the friendly old night owls. Then about 10:30pm or so the far away melody of the coyote.

**Page 7**
Everything would have been OK if old "Spider" Kite hadn't felt sorry for him and gave him that big old warm sheepskin of his. This coupled along with the fact that he had went to visit Joan, the riverboat captain's daughter and almost forgot to come home the night before. Well anyway, Charlie dismounted and settled down in the crotch of the knurled old tree for a vantage point but the warmth of the coat soon lulled him to sleep.

He was rudely awakened by the nuzzling of his horse, about 3:30 in the morning, and he awoke with a guilty start. The morning was crisp, grey and cold just before daybreak, but it was light enough for him to see there wasn't one horse in sight! What to do? Should he ride the two miles into camp and tell them he had fell asleep and lost 750 heard of horses or should he start tracking them alone. He could see it was foolish for him to try and track them alone and soon or later he had to face the music.

Page 8
Well it wasn't exactly music when he got back to camp. However, the thing that bothered Charlie most was the fact that Mr. Groves seemed more worried than mad. Then a little slipped out, it seemed that Grove's knew all the time that "Buck" Rogers and Vince Marcos; two old time horse "competitors" had been following us all the time. Which later turned out to be the true facts of the case. Charlie's stock in trade couldn't have been any lower in camp that morning. Here the men were within about 100 miles of payday and the bonus, and some knot headed kid had let all of the horses go. At the very best making for several weeks of hard riding in hostile Indian country to say the least and the all too evident possibility of facing some horse thieve's gun. After breakfast they broke camp and started to follow the trail which became quite evident was headed south toward the Wyoming Territory.

Page 9
Nine days ride and 350 miles later the men came in sight of the dust of their horses. The scene was quite peaceful, the camp by the spring, and the horses quietly milling around the small lake. With the use of spyglasses Mr. Groves came back with a report that there were seven men, four white and three Mexicans holding them. And his hunch was right. Buck Rogers and Vince Marcos had his horses but hard to get them back. Mr. Groves sent Charlie back to Glendale

to pick up the mail. Most of the men hadn't gotten any for three weeks. Charlie for some reason felt that the might get one from the Grant's. He had been thinking a lot about them since the night of "Big Mistake." Namely the loss of the horses. But he wasn't at all displeased with his mission as there was a good chance he would meet his riverboat girl Maytel.

Page 10
In fact, 10 days ride seemed like a small price to pay to get to see her. The next few days passed quickly with few events out of the ordinary. He rode the ridges, and hogbacks so that he could keep a look out for Indians. He spotted only a few hunting parties at great distance, but never contacted them. Charlie spent one night with a wagon train headed for Canada. This was a real treat to be able to eat some real good home cooked food once more. He was fortunate also in having been able to sleep under a wagon as it hailed some and rained hard all night. When dawn came they were surrounded on three sides by an angry swollen stream, so they broke camp and headed for high ground with no breakfast. Charlie rode slowly until noon without stopping to eat, also giving the streams time to go down......................(Unfinished Story)................

END OF STORY

Vapor Trails
By: Stanley Arden Trollope
Written In
1965-1968

What do I see in a vapor trail?
A life, a jet, a piece of steel.
A time, a place both far and near.
The cage of a loved one,
We hold so dear.

Why do we watch the clear blue sky?
Linger and watch as time goes by.
The large metal object devised by man
For good or evil according to God's plan.

What passes through the mind of a pilot up there?
As he sets the mad pace of his flight through the air.

Does he think of his life or chances of doom, or does he think
Of the bookshelves in his room?

Note:
This is a father's musing in contemplation of his son's military service that
took him far away from the Montana ranch he loved so much. This poem
was written while Dude was flying jets off the aircraft carrier USS Ranger
during the Vietnam War. Setting on a bookshelf above his bed in that old
farmhouse was a plastic model of a Skyhawk fighter jet that he ended up
flying. That model airplane had been placed on that shelf several years before
Dude joined up with the Navy. Was this a coincidence or was it a prophecy?

# Cousin's Contributions

Arla writes:

I remember when Mom & I came to Glendive on the train from Bozeman for Grandma Stockwell's cancer surgery. We were all at the motel near the hospital, Auntie Inez Phillips, Uncle Jim, Auntie Irene, Uncle Frank, Dennis and all of the Wibaux cousins. There was a lot of snow and we went out in the front of that motel and played "Fox & Geese." So much fun! We were all scared for Grandma Stockwell, but we managed to have some "kid fun" anyway. (DT) As sidebar. This took place in about 1949 and Grandma managed to survive not only the cancer but also two strokes finally dying some 25 or 30 years later. She had an iron will and fought all types of maladies. She was determination personified.

In the winter when we went to Grandma & Granddad Stockwell's home, Granddad would always put the corn popper on the stove to pop some corn! Many of us can still hear the popping of the corn while we waited for the last pop.

Arla remembers when Leroy was supposed to be babysitting her when their mom had gone over to Grandma's with Auntie Doris and Auntie Norma to do "assembly line" killing and cleaning of chickens. Leroy was painting their dad's "backhouse". Three-year-old Arla was bored so she told him that she was going over to Grandma's farm but he didn't believe her. She walked pretty far on the way over there, meeting her mom coming home along the way. She was picked up and brought home in a flurry. It is quite possible that Leroy was in trouble for not keeping better tabs on his little sister!! Arla tried it again the next day; however, and then she was in trouble!! Her mom did let her select the stick, which would be used on her posterior as punishment. She picked a very small one but found that even that one hurt a bit.

Remember seeing Arden come down the hill from where the water well was, and he was swinging in full circles two buckets full of water just checking out centrifugal force to see if he could keep the water in the pails!!

Marlene remembers the time when we cousins were having Thanksgiving dinner in the Faltemeyer house in Wibaux. All were seated at a very long table enjoying the feast. It was a special time because Arden was home from the Army having been assigned to Japan in the early 1950's. Marlene asked Arden to pass you the butter and he did? Butter flew through the air directly to Marlene. Her reflexes were admirable as her catch was the finest of the day.

Arden and Arla were driving to Canastota, SD with Grandma and Granddad for those wonderful medical treatments offered there. A stop was made along the way at a roadside stand where watermelons were piled high. Well, Granddad paid for a melon with silver dollars. The vendor at the stand was so mesmerized with the silver dollars that he wanted to exchange some paper currency for the silver dollars. Meanwhile, Arden had put the watermelon in the car. The road stand vendor delivered another watermelon to the car after he got his silver dollars. This made two watermelons the catch of the day. After traveling about ten miles down the road from the produce stand, Granddad said to Arden, "So you bought a melon too?" Arden told him that he had put the watermelon in the car that was purchased and he didn't know that another one was brought to the car. Laughter carried on for many miles until a stop at a park in Canastota where everyone ate plenty of watermelon. This would be one of the "two-fer" sales so common in today's market!

Arla remembers that she and Norrine saw a UFO! Both claim to have seen it so it must have been real.

Arla remembers "swimming in the big tank up at Uncle Roy's farm."

Her dad used to take the kids on wild rides out over the range in the pick up truck. The kids would sit on chairs in the back of the pick up and enjoyed those crazy rides for entertainment.

How about, catching bees in holly hocks . . .

Howard ran for Sheriff six or eight times. Never elected and each time getting fewer votes.

I remember the flying red horses at the CO-OP Oil Station. The gasoline pumps had glass tanks that were filled by using hand pumps to elevate the fuel in precisely measured gallons. Gravity then allowed the gasoline to flow down into the car's gas tank.

The cancellation of gym class because a burning grain elevator was more interesting than a basketball game.

Some would like to forget about driving the red International pickup on the railroad tracks. This was a great feat.

Norrine was in college when her folks brought five-year-old Danny down for a visit. The girls in the dormitory had fun teaching him how to knit. He sat leaning up against the wall out in the hallway and was seen knitting very seriously. Guess it pays to tend to your knitting.

Ronald remembers Leroy and Arden's little toy steam engine. This toy was the hit on every boy's list. It could be used to power Erector Set creations including windmills, and other mechanical innovations.

Horses played a big part in our growing up. Riding Bud while racing with Flash and Tody was a great pass time. Electric fences were used to keep livestock in the corral. It was found that carrying a wet cell battery down to the fence charger while wearing new overalls entailed certain hazards. Leaking acid would bleach and deteriorate the new duds quickly. Loraine also remembers a similar experience as he was sitting on a six-volt wet cell battery used to light the Christmas tree. Oops, there goes another pair of pants.

We had a crazy old goat that was wont to chase us kids every chance that he got especially when we were walking unprotected in the middle of the corral.

Sleeping in the bunkhouse reading Big Little books was a great time for us.

Picking sunburn scabs off Arden's back to help relieve the itching sensations was a duty that always proved to be fun for all.

Eating cottage cheese that Auntie Maye made (small curds) was something we all looked forward to.

Riding on the drawbar of the International Model B tractor-getting water was looked forward to by everyone. There were times when the front end of that little tractor would rise up off the ground to a height of four feet. Haying down on Section 31 was a family task also. A Farm Hand and buck rakes were used to gather and move the newly mowed hay, which was put up in stacks for winter livestock feed. All of the time we were watching for rattlesnakes since some of this work took place during the "dog days" of summer when snakes skins are shed over their heads obscuring their sight. At this time of the year they would be likely to strike at any movement or sound.

Drinking water out of the spring at Reuben's ranch was a treat. The water was cold but didn't taste real good.

Then there were the times when harvest brought big dinners of fried chicken when our Wisconsin relatives were around to help out.

Grinding horseradishes on a very windy day at Grandma and Granddad Stockwell's place. We used the little green bench they had.

Sitting on the steep open narrow steps eating Christmas dinner at Granddad's and afterwards playing FLINCH.

Watching Granddad eat peas with a knife with honey on it.

Sitting on his lap playing with that pocket watch.

How about that old leather rocker he would sit in.

The Servel refrigerators I think they bought them in Bozeman. Granddad, Reuben and Roy's all had one. First refrigerator at the Roy Amunrud home had an electric cord to power the interior light. Problem was that they did not have an electrical outlet. Ronald used to have to empty the pan under the old icebox and then go to the machine shed to get ice out of the sawdust it was packed in to fill up the icebox again.

Norma Amunrud made homemade root beer in the basement.

Watching rancher Wilson race by in his new cars.

Gathering eggs in the dark when getting home late.

Running home to listen to the Lone Ranger at 4:30pm. Could only use the radios a half hour because those hot packs cost one dollar.

Granddad Stockwell would get tears in his eyes laughing at the antics that were observed on the farm. You all remember that. Granddad was a happy man. Never saw him mad. He maybe should have been mad when Ronald drove the International B tractor under the sagging Blue Mountain telephone line at the farm. Damage to the tractor included bent booms. Sure felt bad about that.

Grandma took Ronald hunting deer south of their house.

Riding in a sleigh up to Ed Volendorf's place after a big storm. And Leroy being pulled on skis with a rope.

Parties at the Cottonwood Hall with Stanley Trollope acting like Jackie Gleason, the comedian on TV, and we had to guess who he was imitating.

Alvin Trollope, what a nice kid.

John Trollope's new four door slant back '49 Chevy.

Roy Amunruud's new gas W-9 International tractor. It could pull anything.

The time coming from school and side swiping Granddad and Grandma's Lincoln Cosmopolitan on the schoolhouse hill. It's a wonder no one was hurt.

Eating or trying to eat a cottontail rabbit that Granddad shot when snowed in at their place in '49.

Sleeping in that feather bed in their house.

Norrine writes about using dandelions placed under your chin to see if you liked butter or not.

Riding two little Shetland ponies to Granddad & Grandma's house for sugar cookies and to play with all of the baby kittens.

Trips down in Grandma's root cellar for a jar of peaches or something Grandma requested and finding lizards down there. Loraine can remember one occasion in which a rattlesnake was lying on the cellar doorframe just at head level. He did not strike. Lucky!

Cousin Norrine remembers bringing the ponies into the house and braiding their tails and manes. Her mom was so nervous while they were in the house. She never wanted a dog or cat in the house but did let the horses in.

And then there were the hundreds of birthday parties and card parties that brought us cousins together to play all over the place.

The haymow in Uncle Johnnie's (Trollope) barn was always fun to play in, as was the Roy Amunrud barn with all of the rafters to crawl on and then jump off into the stored grain. Roy Amunrud (Daddy) did not like the kids jumping in the grain, though.

Norrine would ride down to play with Arla where they played with dolls and had tea parties. Auntie Maye enjoyed it as much as the girls did. They would ride horses, Pet & Toady, all over the place.

The pitchfork fondues down there were also so much fun. I sure hope they cleaned the pitchforks good before the big meal!!

Norrine remembers playing with the Wyckoff girls in the water that accumulated in the road ditches after a rain and catching pollywogs and squishing them between their fingers.

It was fun to play house in the very tall pigweeds and play hide and seek there.

Remember the huge hole that we dug with spoons.

We finally got permission to sleep outside over night out there. It took several trips from the house to get it all setup comfortably. We got all bedded down for the night when Daddy got to thinking that if the cows got out, they just may step on top of the blankets and boards that had been placed across the top and would fall through. He came out and made us go to the house.

Remember Arla when we were sitting in the outhouse at our place and we saw a UFO. Leroy questioned me about that the other day.

Shelly remembers riding horses to some pond, puddle or slough? Anyway, while at the Lunde's we were playing in the water and somehow a pollywog got in my T-shirt and got squished in my armpit . . . eewww! Clint or Craig do you know how it got there? I have always wondered how that happened.

Naomi, do you remember that day? I also remember riding triple on Missy up the big hill from the house to the corral. Unfortunately, I was in the back and slid right off of her rear end rolling down the hill. It was always exciting to visit the farm especially when we got to bottle feed the lambs and gather eggs. Those roosters were mean though.

Another treasured memory is riding on the tailgate of Gordon's old blue pickup and picking up straw bales. A few years later, I remember Naomi driving the pickup and we saw a rattlesnake in the road and had to back up so we could drive over it back and forth until we knew it was dead. I remember on our trips to Wibaux from Sidney. There always was a spot between Glendive and Wibaux next to the highway were we would check in the spring for crocuses blooming.

What about watermelon eating and seed spitting contests . . . any of you remember doing that. Orange Crush and Grape soda in bottles were a special treat at the gas station on the corner in Wibaux when we went to town.

Arden writes of his memories: Hot beef sandwiches at George's Café.

Wonderful soft (albeit brown) water from Uncle Roy's.

Jumping into wheat from the machine shed rafters after crawling through the bowels of Uncle Johnnie's threshing machine.

The threshing crews with the trapezoidal hay racks for unloading the bundles into the feeder.

Riding bareback and using pig weed "spears" while playing cowboys and Indians.

Taking cover under a tractor when hail is "harvesting" a good crop.

Going 50 MPH in Uncle Roy's Model A Ford. Sleeping on wet hay. The labor/energy saving forklift on the F-30.

Fourth of July picnic at Stockwell's.

Beaver dams near the Airdrome. Pancakes with Gilbertsons on Section 31.

The strawberry shortcakes using Wisconsin berries. Blue teeth after eating choke cherries.

Opening many gates just to go to Sidney's Richland County Fair the short way. Riding the Ferris wheel at the fair with Ronald.

Climbing the sand rocks at Blue Mountain.

Waking up to rain pounding on the bunkhouse roof.

Sun burns every spring.

Helvik's grocery, gas and shoe repair.

Walking over the curved top iron bridge going to the Davis addition in Wibaux. The wood walkway along the creek & the swimming holes. Going under the viaduct when a train went over. Riding bikes up both sides (East & West) of the overpass.

Huge icicles hanging from the railroad water tank.

Ice skating across from the church.

Adding a little string so I could yoyo from the top of the school.

Riding on the fenders of the 1936 Ford. Using the lights as "pretend" steering wheel.

Going south over the "stomach raising" bump by the "Lone Tree."

Marlene writes of her memories:
Staying overnight at Granddad & Grandma's home with those pretty quilts and the chamber pot under the bed.

Those stair steps where we sat to eat at big family dinners.

Granddad at breakfast putting Puffed Wheat in his cereal bowl and saying, "Mmm shot from guns" then spilling cereal all over the table. Grandma wasn't too happy but us kids sure did laugh.

Marlene remembers playing in the bloody turkey feathers on those cold days in November before Thanksgiving.

Grandma sewed new aprons for her daughters out of chicken feed sacks.

Yes, the big leather rocking chair. Irene was sitting in it and I crawled up on her lap and said, "I like to sit on your big fat lap."

Grandma wondering what happened to her cats after Loraine, Alvin & Dude had been there and put them in a cream can with the lid on.

Getting up early to go to Uncle Johnny's barn fire and watching it burn.

Cousin's photos at Welch's studio in Beach.

Charley Dalthorp in his little old pick up brought a refrigerator, Shetland pony 'Hepcat' and a new bicycle to Wibaux for us after we bought them all in Bozeman in 1947 or'48.

Boys all putting their skis together we sat on them and slid down hill during recess at our one room school. Mr. Leland was the teacher.

Fred Vollendorf stopping to visit Reuben fixing fence and didn't know who he was after he had all of his teeth pulled.

Buying nickel strawberry pop at the Sidney fair and the store in Skaar.

Ronald and Arden on the Ferris wheel in Beach. Ronald trying to jump out and Arden holding him in. Mom & Maye standing there telling the attendant to STOP.

Mick singing Zippity Do Da all the way from Forsyth to our place after he had seen the movie.

Duane and his magic tricks. He was good.

Norrine and I milking early so we could go to a movie in Beach and a cow got tangled up in the milker. I saw Uncle Johnny coming over the 'school house' hill and ran and flagged him down. He had Thomse with him and he parked right by our outhouse, as Ray needed to get to one while Johnny untangled the cow from the milking machine. I think Ray had a broken leg.

It was always fun to have the O'Connor kids come and play.

Every chance 'Honey' (Trollope's Shetland) got she ran to our place and they would come and get her, tie her to the bumper and lead he back home. "Honey" was a sister to our good old "Pet", who died at age 28.

We stayed in town for school when 'Rainey' was in the first grade. He stayed with us in one room at Marvin Bushman's house. (Dennis remembers sleeping in the closet on an army cot next to the electric hot plate used to cook our meals. This was the first time I remember eating cold cereal from small cardboard boxes lined with waxed paper.)

That was the year Grandma got cancer and Granddad came to tell us and he cried. She was tough like we all are and survived that. Grandma did finally die—some 25 or 30 years later.

Oh yes, Big Babies. Leroy was 12 pounds; Norrine born at home, 11 pounds; Marlene weighed 8 pounds four ounces and Willy three months younger weighed almost four pounds at birth. Auntie Olive always told Mom she ate too many potatoes! When Mom was in labor with me, Auntie Edna kept telling her to hold off until after midnight so I would be a leap year baby! Edna thought I was born 6 hours too soon! Mom didn't.

Dennis planted his wheat crop out in the yard over by Joe and Merle's farm that fall. Granddad had some wheat in the hopper and went and cut Dennis's crop. Wow, was he tickled when he saw all of that wheat! I think Dennis should have remained a farmer. He was a cute little kid, wasn't he?

It was a great trip and I wouldn't trade it for anything! Marlene.

Arden remembers electioneering with Granddad Stockwell:
We were near Golva and went by a farmhouse that was still smoldering from a fire that burned it down to nothing. I have no idea whose it was. Granddad Stockwell was passing out cards and meeting people. That's all I remember.

Arla remembers:
Arla remembers that Grandma & Granddad Stockwell's mechanical toys that they received from the Gilbertson's every Christmas.

Grandma letting us drink coffee with sugar and cream in it out of one of her little cups.

Grandma's baked beans.

When we lived in Omaha we went over to Loraine and Joyce's for Thanksgiving dinner. They had a decorated cream can and Loraine told us that they had scoured the countryside to find that cream can and paid $7.00 for it. He said, "Arla, how many times have I eaten Thanksgiving dinner sitting on a cream can with a catalog on it to make it more "comfortable"?

I used to drive over to Grandma's to get some of their soft water (in cream cans) to wash our hair with on Saturday night and after they got a TV set, I would try to go when "The Lawrence Welk Show" was on. Mom, Auntie Doris, Auntie Norma, Grandma and sometimes Auntie Nett, most of them with dishtowels tied around their heads as they washed.

The occasions when they met on a Saturday afternoon in Wibaux having pie and coffee at that little restaurant where the Wibaux Paper is now. I think. Then there was always the fight over who was going to pay the bill. One time I remember Auntie Nett walked out and threw money over her shoulder as she walked out the door!

Grandma, Granddad and Mom drove me down to Omaha when I went to college there. That was a brave move as none of us had ever been in the state of Nebraska before and I was 17 years old (soon to be 18) going to a big city where I didn't know anyone. Our trusted family Dr. Olson had gone to Creighton University in Omaha for his medical training, and he told us that we needed to get a pizza when we were there. Grandma did whatever Dr. Olson told her to do, so when we arrived, we asked at Grace (my college) there was a good pizza place. We went to Oddo's and Mom, Grandma and I each ordered a pizza!! Granddad ordered his usual fried egg sandwich or grilled cheese-I don't recall which—and he really laughed when he saw those three whole pizzas. Well, you know we were not to waste any food, and Grandma was entered in Methodist Hospital the next day!! She really was in the hospital for about three days, and it was so confusing as Mom was trying to drive around Omaha from the hospital to the college to the hotel and taking care of Granddad and shopping for bedspreads, curtains, etc. for my dorm room. That was our introduction to pizza.

Salmon sandwiches made on homemade bread, with butter and lettuce.

I sure miss having some input here from Dude!

Lyla writes:

I don't remember Uncle Dan ever running for Sheriff but that doesn't mean he didn't. Could have been before my time.

Yes my dad, Howard, was sheriff of Golden Valley Country for a couple of terms in the 30's & 40's and also deputy for a couple of terms.

Marlene writes:
I remember Uncle Len in his bib overalls. I don't know where he slept at Granddads as Jeanette was still home (graduated in 1944) when he lived with them. They didn't have a bunkhouse.

John D. built Granddad Stockwell's new garage and with the scraps of lumber he built a new outhouse right beside it. We bought the outhouse at their auction and used it for ten years before we built our house with running water and a bathroom. The outhouse still sits in our pasture where we moved it for an all day school activity years ago. The garage was moved to their house in town and is still being used.

# HERE WE ARE!

Back Row: Ronald Amunrud Leroy Amunrud Arden Amunrud
Middle Row: Norrine Amunrud Marlene Amunrud Arla Amunrud
Front Row: Alvin Trollope Loraine Trollope Dennis Stockwell
Seated: Duane Trollope
Circa: 1943